Thank you very much.
May God Bless You.
~ Robin K.

662 231-2918

Thank You for
ending homelessness!!
Verghor.

901
218
0496

Writing Our Way Home

A Group Journey Out of Homelessness

by

RODERICK BALDWIN

DONNA CONNIE

CYNTHIA CRAWFORD

JACQUELINE CROWDER

VEYSHON HALL

TAMARA HENDRIX

WILLIAM L. HOGAN, JR.

LATASHA JACKSON

ANTHONY JOHNSTON

ROBBIN K.

RHONDA LAY

JOCKLUSS THOMAS PAYNE

LEROY SCOTT

WJS

MASTER MAJOR JOSHUA WILLIAMS

RODERICK BALDWIN
DONNA CONNIE
CYNTHIA CRAWFORD
JACQUELINE CROWDER
VEYSHON HALL
TAMARA HENDRIX
WILLIAM L. HOGAN, JR.

A GROUP JOURNEY OUT OF HOMELESSNESS

LATASHA JACKSON
ANTHONY JOHNSTON
ROBBIN K.
RHONDA LAY
JOCKLUSS THOMAS PAYNE
LEROY SCOTT
W JS
MASTER MAJOR JOSHUA WILLIAMS

Cover Design by Connor Covert
Art Direction by Maggie White
Cover Art and Interior Art by Allison Lawyer
Back Cover Art by Jockluss Thomas Payne

Published by

Triton Press
A division of The Nautilus Publishing Company
426 S. Lamar Blvd., Suite 16
Oxford, MS 38655
Tel: 662-513-0159
www.TritonPressHybrid.com

ISBN: 978-1-936946-30-3

PRINTED IN THE UNITED STATES OF AMERICA

WHAT THEY ARE SAYING

When you open your copy of *WRITING OUR WAY HOME: A GROUP JOURNEY OUT OF HOMELESSNESS* by writers from Memphis' Door of Hope writing group, do so with absolutely no preconceived notions because every page, story, anecdote, poem, and observation will surprise you. Sincere, raw, intelligent, and sometimes downright laugh-out-loud hilarious, this collection of writings is not so much about the issue of homelessness as it is about life and the world as seen through the eyes of beautiful people who happen to have been affected by homelessness. From politics and the national debt, to vegetarianism, nature, addiction, and Elvis Presley, the insight to be gained from these writers is rare, fascinating, and ultimately a reward to experience. Everyone should read this book.

> Tim Sampson
> Founding editor *The Memphis Flyer*
> Former editor *MEMPHIS* magazine
> Communications Director Soulsville Foundation

United Methodist Bishop Ken Carder once told me that it was just as dangerous to the spiritual life to have no contact with the poor as to have no contact with the sacrament. He also said a sacrament is an outward sign of an inner grace. This book is a sacrament. Read these stories of baptism, confession and confirmation from the Door of Hope Writing Group and hear God speak.

> David Waters
> Columnist for *The Commercial Appeal* in Memphis

Writing Our Way Home allows us to hear from a segment of our society that is too often ignored. Get ready to have your soul pierced, your heart uplifted and your understanding of homelessness expanded.

The Memphis School of Servant Leadership

WRITING OUR WAY HOME is significant in many ways. First, the idea behind it is brilliant...giving people who go unnoticed in so many ways THE OPPORTUNITY to express themselves in their own way, for their own sake. The originators of the project know the power of words. If you don't, you will as you read this book. I can't imagine an emotion that will not be touched, and in many cases, lead to action...at least change your ideas and assumptions about a population that needs to be recognized, affirmed, and cared for.

Saying something, especially if you put it in writing, makes what you say real. In fact, some things don't become real until they are expressed. So these writers, homeless persons, have written their way home because home is knowing who you are, expressing who you are, and having others to know you as you are. I could not commend the book more highly.

Maxie Dunnam
Director, Christ Church Global
Co-Host of *We Believe in Memphis*

I found this work to be riveting, revealing, and powerful.
Phil Darius Wallace
Writer and producer of one-man show on the life of
Martin Luther King, Malcolm X, and
Frederick Douglass

I have had the pleasure and privilege of writing with the Door of Hope writing group and I have found true inspiration in their midst. Weekly, the writers have shared from the heart of their lives, exposing their vulnerability, pain and fear as well as their sense of humor, joy and pride.

These stories open a door of hope for all of us as they show us how to nurture our dreams even when our dreaming is no longer sheltered by walls and a roof over our head. I invite you to walk into these stories and find yourself a place to belong among these gracious and generous writers.

Elaine Blanchard
Prison Stories Creator and Coordinator
www.ElaineBlanchard.com

This book, and the tales contained within it, are proof that both life and love will endure in the harshest of conditions. It serves as a message of hope to all who read it, for if love can still spring forth in those who have suffered so much, there is hope for all of us in this world.

Aaron Banks
Editor-at-Large, *The Bridge: The Memphis Street Paper*

People on the streets have stories to tell. They have varied histories, hopes, and dreams even in the midst of sharing the condition of being homeless. This collection of stories written by those who have experienced homelessness is poignant, compelling, and startling. The writers are refreshingly honest, sometimes poetic, and always truth-tellers about their lives. If you want to learn something of the powerful humanity of those on the streets and the gritty realities they face with courage, wisdom, hope, and humor, this is an excellent place to start.

Pete Gathje
Co-Director, Manna House
Professor of Christian Ethics at Memphis Theological
Seminary

In reading these writings, I was touched, challenged, educated, encouraged, surprised and much more. I think it is significant that all of these voices are going to be heard through this book. I look forward to buying a copy and sharing it with others.

Thank you and all the writers for offering this gift to the community.

Kristin Fox-Trautman
Memphian

When we think about homelessness, many of us recall the common stereotypes society has placed on our unsheltered brothers and sisters. However, when we get to know the stories and experiences of the men and women who have actually lived through it, we are reminded that homelessness is a unique and complex situation and that those who have been without a safe place to call home are not entirely defined by that experience. They are our brothers and sisters, friends, family, veterans, but most importantly, people with valuable stories and experiences to share. I have worked side by side with authors of this publication; men and women with a passion for changing public perceptions about homelessness and working to shine light on the plight of those whose voices are often marginalized. There is strength, inspirational power, and hope in the pages of this book!

Paul Garner
Organizing Coordinator, (HOPE) Homeless Organizing
for Power & Equality, Memphis, TN

What a gift Ellen has given to the writers and to the community. We all have a story, and to have it heard and validated is very transformative. Our stories are what we can hold onto so we never want to forget the past or close the door on it. Sometimes it is in the telling of our story that we find the grace to carry on and move in a different direction. Thanks for allowing me to be a small part of this journey with the group. It has been transformative for me as well.

Onie Johns
Founder/Director Caritas Village

It is a gift to read stories that bind us together in the transformative power of love. Writing Our Way Home is a mosaic of stories that bridge divides and remind us all of our deep connections. The writings of the participants in the Door of Hope writing group create a composite of a life moving into, through and out of homelessness told through 15 distinctive voices that call us to compassion. These autobiographical stories give authentic voice to the challenges, setbacks, joys and hopes of the journey of trying to find our way home through writing.

Rev. Becca Stevens

Founder of Magdalene and Thistle Farms

Author of *Snake Oil: The Art of Healing and Truth-Telling* and *The Way of Tea & Justice: Rescuing the World's Favorite Beverage From Its Violent History* (Fall 2014)

INTRODUCTION

I was seated in the living room of a lovely Craftsman cottage, attending class. The class was offered by the Memphis School of Servant Leadership. About six of us were scattered on the sofa, chairs, and ottomans. During class, I had been talking so much about writing that one of the other students, Rev. Joe Porter, finally looked at me and said, "Ellen, you talk so much about writing. You should go to the Door of Hope and start a writing group."

The Memphis School of Servant Leadership asks its students to form relationships with those who have been pushed to the margins of society. I hadn't figured out a way to do this that didn't feel artificial, condescending ... just fulfilling a class requirement. When Joe mentioned a writing group, I saw a way. In writing group, we all come to the table as equals. We all come as writers.

I went to the Door of Hope, an organization described on its website as "dedicated to ending homelessness, one door at a time." I thought I would walk in, receive a list of policies, tour the facility, and generally ease into this new venture. Instead, I wandered through a house and into its backyard, the backyard being where the Door of Hope met at the time. Dr. June Averyt, the Founding Executive Director of Door of Hope, called to those seated on picnic tables, "This is Ellen Prewitt! She's gonna tell us how to be a writing group!"

I'd been a member of many writing groups, but I'd never started one before. I certainly knew nothing about "working with the homeless." Thankfully, June's approach didn't give me time to think about any of that. Everyone migrated to one picnic table. I sat down, and we talked.

Leroy Scott, one of our founding members, asked a lot of questions; Leroy, with his deep Barry White voice, was a leader in the group from the beginning. Because it was Wednesday, we decided we would meet on Wednesdays. I would bring paper and pencils. We would write and see how it went. For almost seven years, we've been following that routine: meeting on Wednesdays, writing, seeing how it goes.

Writing group has followed the Door of Hope from the backyard picnic tables to a yellow brick church on Monroe Avenue into the coffee-and-sunlight-drenched Support Center on North Bellevue Avenue. Here, Roderick Baldwin, one of the founders of our group, presides as Support Center Manager. Sometimes members of the greater Memphis community who have no personal experience of homelessness join us. Since October, 2011, we've been joined on our journey by the clergy and staff at Germantown United Methodist Church. These folks began as guests of the group, joining us to write. Now, when life takes me out of town, they facilitate the group. They host us on field trips; they've been instrumental in bringing this book to life. They have become not just valued members of the group, but our angels as well.

Over the years, hundreds of people have written with the writing group. Some have come to us as beautiful writers—you will see this in the work of Tommy Payne, one of our founding members. Others are more like me, learning to write one sentence at a time. Some writers were with us briefly; others joined us for a month or two or three—as long as they needed—then moved on. Others were like Robb Pate, who wrote with us from the founding of the group until he was no longer on this earth.

The life of writing group has been full. Guest authors have come talk to us. We've held three public readings; we've hosted four Annual Community Writing Retreats where the public paid to attend day-long series of workshops co-led by a published author and a Door of Hope writer. We've produced and sold notecards. For almost three years, we published a monthly ezine, *The Advocate: A Voice of Experience,* featuring the writers as paid contributors. All of this the writers accomplished while simultaneously pursuing their journey off the street, into a shelter, into housing. Into a home.

Several years ago, the idea of a writing group book began to take hold. In 2012, this culminated in a Book Retreat at Germantown United Methodist Church where the then-members of writing group reviewed their folders and selected the writings they wanted to include in the book. I structured these writings into sections and chapters. Volunteer editors met with each writer and reviewed his or her writings. Gradually, the book came together.

As you read the resulting book, here are a few pieces of information you might find helpful.

"Homelessness" is a continuum. Over the years, some folks have come to writing group after spending the night on the streets. Some were staying at overnight missions. Some had been accepted into temporary shelters. Others were newly housed in their own apartments. Gradually, folks move along this continuum. Only when safely ensconced in their own place do folks become "housed."

The Door of Hope is a nonprofit organization founded in 2003 by what its website describes as a core group of Memphians, Midtown Memphis churches, and area non-profits who wanted to address homelessness in their Midtown neighborhood. The purpose of the Door of Hope is to "provide a welcoming place where people living on the streets may come to learn healthy living skills and to build positive relationships with people." More of the organization's history can be found at doorofhopememphis.org.

We begin weekly writing group by discussing a topic for the day. The topic is brought by me, the other facilitators, or a member of the group—William L. Hogan, Jr., one of our founding members, frequently brings topics. We discuss the topic, noting any writing exercises imbedded therein, and then we're quiet as folks write. All are free to write on topic or to write about whatever is in their hearts or on their minds. When we're finished, we take turns sharing our work or we choose to keep it private.

The entries in this book are presented in chronological chapters exploring periods in the writers' lives (e.g., When We Were Young, As We Grew Up.) The entries were not written chronologically. The stories contained herein are the writers' stories of their lives as they perceive them. As you read through the book, you will note that the understanding of certain experiences and life in general shifts over time as the writers—like all of us—gain new insights or wisdom. You will also notice the status of Dr. June Averyt as Executive Director of Door of Hope changed, but her involvement in the writers' lives continued; we are pleased to include her note to the writers in the Acknowledgement page.

Some writers who are in the book have been members of writing group longer than others; consequently, you will see more of their work. If space permitted, we would have added other excellent chapters such as, Responding to Tragedy, but space did not permit.

As you read the book, you'll learn from the experts the answers to questions you might have about homelessness—what is it like to live in a shelter? Did you use soup kitchens? What was your daily routine? How did you become homeless? Who were you before you were homeless? Through their own words, the writers will tell you about themselves. You will hear much talk about God. You will read strong political or philosophical opinions with which you might disagree. You will hear some tough stories that take courage to share; we hope you will honor the bravery present in the telling. You will read how writing group fit into the fabric of people's lives as they worked to move forward from a long process of becoming homeless into a long process of becoming housed. Most important, you will learn the answer to the question: who are you now?

Ellen Morris Prewitt
Door of Hope Writing Group co-facilitator

FOREWORD

Over my forty-three years of pastoral ministry I've had many experiences in which God awakened me anew to the blessings which come in unsuspecting and surprising ways. We can call these serendipitous moments or God-sent experiences, but they are those sacred times when you find yourself absolutely blessed beyond belief and expectation.

Such has been our journey with the Door of Hope Writing Group. As Ellen Prewitt notes in her introduction, we came to know the writers in this group and began our special time together in October 2011. What she doesn't mention is that it happened when some of us staff persons at Germantown Methodist were invited to sit in on a writing session while carrying out a staff team building experience. The graciousness and love with which we were immediately received was remarkable! We were allowed into their stories and their lives, not as strangers but as friends. That sense of friendship and caring connection continues to this day.

As we continue to hear their stories and listen to their writings, we find our lives touched, our souls enriched, and our faith enhanced. These participants in the Door of Hope Writing Group have experienced challenges and setbacks in life which would send many a person of faith reeling and make many persons grow angry and jaded. We don't experience that with these our friends. They are honest about their disappointments and their struggles, but they are also expressive of faith in God and how He enables courage amidst great challenges.

I can categorically say that they inspire us more than we ever can inspire them.

It is also pure joy at times to be on outings with these participants and hear their laughter, their jokes, their loving jabbing of each other; and even of us. What a witness; keeping and exuding joy when it would be so easy to do otherwise.

We staff persons at Germantown Methodist consider it one of our richest blessings to continue to be a part of this special group of people and to partner with Ellen for continuing meaningful stories!

Richard Smith
Senior Pastor
Germantown United Methodist Church

PART I
BEFORE WE WERE HOMELESS

CHAPTER 1
WHEN WE WERE YOUNG

I started drawing cartoons when I was about five years old. I also helped my mom at raising flowers. I was good at trapping small animals and catching snakes and nutria rats, plus getting butt whippings for venturing off into the woods where no one knew where I was.

Tommy Payne

A special place for me takes me back to my childhood. It was under my baby brother's baby bed. I used to sit under his bed and put a sheet in front of it. I used to pretend it was my own little house. It was my little hideaway. I would sit under there for hours, and play all by myself. In my own imaginary world, I used to like it because I was quiet and peaceful. I could go there and be in my own little world.

Latasha Jackson

Growing up in Memphis for me was very interesting. I had 3 sisters, my mother and father. We were originally from Buffalo, New York and moved here when I was about 6 years old. I fell in love with the weather instantly. Because it was much warmer than New York. There was a lot of peach trees and pear trees and pecan trees. People had gardens in their back yards. Back in the '50s and '60s Memphis was known as the City of Good Abode! And one of the cleanest cities in America.

So, in short, growing up in Memphis has been a totally awesome trip.

Leroy Scott

Well, growing up in the city, my mother was my backbone and she was everything to me when she was living. I grew up with 5 brothers and no sisters. I was the only girl, so me and my mom became close, just like sisters. She taught me to be the woman I am today. She taught me to be strong and voice my opinions: right and wrongs. The whoopings she gave me and the wet towel whoopings made me respect myself as an adult and trust people like you want to be trusted. I constantly think of my mother. She was a God-fearing woman and taught me things that I never would imagine. As I look back on things like going to Bible Sunday school and church on Wednesday, Saturday, and Sunday, my mother was planting the seed of Jesus in my heart and soul.

I thank God for my beautiful mother. Now I realize I am just like her in so many ways. I thank the Lord for her and now I pass down my old spirit to my daughters as my mother did me.

Robbin K

Momma don't go! What about me! A child of three.

"Child I have to go to work."

What's your nighttime excuse, Mama!

"You stay here with him."

A child of abuse. Years pass with no attention or concern for me. I'm dying inside. Why am I not like other kids? No playtime, no sleepovers or bedtime prayers. I want to be accepted and loved! Is that so hard or too much to ask? Momma he's touching me. Momma he hurt me.

"Child, why are you saying these things?" But you're my mom, don't you want to protect me?

"Child you're lying." Momma, I feel like I'm dying.

TRUTH! Lies. LIES! Truth. Mom, what about me? I'm your baby.

"Child, what about him, he would never." But I'm your baby.

"I love him." Don't you love me, Momma?

I called the police. He hurt me! "He would never." But he did. "She just needs to be told you love her, that's all." She does not love me. She loves him. When I'm told the truth is a lie and a lie is the truth. What do I do, what do I know? The abuse is horrible, but it's all I know!

Cynthia Crawford

It's amazing that as a child, I didn't have to earn for anything. Things turned out good when I did what I was told; when I didn't it wasn't good. I was placed in an all white school and it turned out pretty good. I met some good classmates, even though there was some who didn't want us there! I made it out. It turned out good for me because of all the health problems I was having. It turned out better because I was willing to do what they told me to do to stay healthy. Being sincere in asking God for help has given me the Spirit of helping self and treating others the way I want to be treated! I feel I turned out O.K. There is hope.

Roderick Baldwin

I was with my family I was comfortable and not having to question myself about where I would be living. I could find work in the area and it was easy for me to bus or drive to and from work. The caring about me and what I did and did not do meant the world too. Had the run of the house, they saw to it that I had the time of life of a life-time every day. Family cares.

Master Major Joshua Williams

I was born in a small town called Wrightsville, Georgia to loving parents. Raised in Atlanta, Georgia, the capitol city, and graduated from George Washington Carver Comprehensive High School. I had an A, B grade average thru high school. I graduated at the age of 16. I entered high school at the age of 11.

WJS

Me and my brother Bobby will sometime go to our friends on their vacation and on Easter we hunt eggs and have fun. Before we hunt, he has a little sister, we watch her hunt and then the older parts of the family will hide the eggs and we hunt and then eat.

Anthony Johnston

One day I was playing in the front yard, when I decided that I was going to roller skate. I put my skates on and began to skate up and down the street. Everything was fine until I slid and fell hard to the ground. In a sleepy haze, all I could remember was my family running around trying to pick me up and calling my name. They sounded so far away. All I could see for a while was lights all around me. The next thing I knew, I was on the couch and my uncle was shaking me to wake me up. I was so sleepy. Then I was in my aunt's car on the way to the children's hospital. Finally the doctor checked me out and I had a broken arm. I was lucky that I didn't sustain a concussion, he said. The doctor wrapped my arm and fit me for a cast. I know it could have been worse. I was up and running in about another month.

Tamara Hendrix

I can remember when I followed the sign of waiting for the spring weather. When spring started then there would be rain. That was when I was young on up until I grew old. I would feel that I could go out in the rain and the water would serve me the weather I was looking for. I wanted the heavy rain the have a not raining space for me. I would feel that the rain had did its job to deliver water on the dry things and this occasion would say a wet day on the dry of the surroundings and it would be a surprise—the dry would get back after a rain. I always waited for the dry to be again. I always was happy when the rain stopped and the dry would reappear.

William L. Hogan, Jr.

The year was 1963 and President John F. Kennedy had gotten assassinated in Dallas TX. On a rainy Friday afternoon about 1:00 central time, I can still see Walter Cronkite saying that on TV. I was in the sixth grade and my teacher told the class that President Kennedy had been shot and we were shocked pretty bad because we weren't used to that type of violence. She told us that it was an attempted assassination. And we discussed it to get a feeling of it. Later that day, people were crying and the skies were crying and it was just a very sad atmosphere.

Leroy Scott

My grandmother raised fruits and vegetables. In addition to that she also raised chickens, ducks, turkeys and other farm animals. My grandfather raised Appaloosas ponies for a race track called Louisiana Downs. Outside of being a farmer's paradise, Lake Charles, Louisiana was a gambling city. Even drugstores had slot machines.

Most of the vegetables my grandmother raised were sold. I was in charge of the selling. I was about 14 years old. Watermelons, cantaloupes, squash, okra, purple hull peas, and other food items filled my pickup truck which I drove underage and without a license.

I was a very energetic and industrious child. "Country" as people would call me in this era. This was a memorable time in my young life. I used to go fishing at least once or twice a week. My special place would be the wildflowers and backwaters of the Red River outside of Lake Charles, Louisiana. I spent many peaceful days fishing on the river and enjoying the pleasant scenery. It was like nostalgia, just an exquisite feeling of being this close to nature and god.

Today, I yet raise gardens at Door of Hope. I also do spices. Most of all, I sell paintings in my fading years. I'm just about the same person I was then.

Tommy Payne

I always loved Christmas when I was a child. I loved when it was time to decorate the Christmas tree. I liked getting the decorations out. We would sort everything out. We would put the tree up. Then we would work with the lights and get them working. Next we would put on the bulbs. Then we would put the icicles on one by one. Then we would put the star on top. After we finished we would go outside to see how pretty it was.

Latasha Jackson

At home we put up one big Christmas tree with fixings. My Dad does all the work, with presents all around, with the star shining on top. As a child I remember the shining star.

Master Major Joshua Williams

I was around twelve or thirteen years old and it was a New Year's Day, one very cold January day. I was walking down the street in my neighborhood and this elderly lady, one of my favorites, asked me to come in her house and walk around her house in every room.

Back then and even now people had a thing about a man being the first person in their house, the reason being that it was to bring you good luck. So that day I ended up walking through about 15-20 houses and made myself a nice little piece of money. I was thankful and they were also.

Leroy Scott

The Valentine's Day in my family was a special day for me. Valentine's Day is my brother's and mother's birthdays. I cry a lot because I miss my mother. God bless her soul.

Jacqueline Crowder

I was a leader when I was a boy scout. I was recently a leader in home basketball. A one who leads and this is what it means to me.

William L. Hogan, Jr.

I love peaches! I can eat them by themselves, in a pie, made into preserves, etc. I remember there was a peach tree in my backyard. I would love to climb just to pick the peaches off. I would gather them, excluding the ones the worms ate holes in, and bring them to my grandmother so she could make a cobbler for dinner. My job was to wash them and cut them up into halves so they could be smashed into a mixture to go in the pie. I would always sneak and eat one, tasting the sweet citrusy texture of the peaches. Now that I'm grown up, I shop at the market or supermarket for fresh peaches.

Tamara Hendrix

I was born in St. Louis, MO by Reola and Bob K. My father was a welder and my mother was a homemaker. As a child, me and my brothers went to church often and, in the summer, went to Day Camp when school was out. Nine years went by and we moved to a place called Flint, Michigan in 1975. I was 9 years old. As a child, me and my brothers were very athletic. My oldest brother was a wrestler, second oldest was a baseball player, and the third oldest brother was a track star and the twins were football players and cross country runners. I was a honor roll student in high school and worked as a senior at a warehouse distribution center.

Robbin K

I wipe the nervous sweat from my brow as I look out across the landscape. I take one big gulp of air and then exhale expectantly. Suddenly, I hear the cheerful laughter of children in the nearby field. Running, jumping, and playing against the backdrop of trees, fields, and flowers. As a gentle breeze blows leaves all about, I smell a subtle hint of honeysuckle in the air. Then the clang, clang, clang of the ice cream truck's bells dominating over the wind. I run to jump on the swing but miss and am knocked face first into the sand by another kid swinging. I raise up as tears well in my big brown eyes and spit out the gritty salty tasting sand.

Oh! How I want to cry, but wait, it's Mama picking me up, dusting me off.

"Don't cry, baby. Don't be afraid, Mommy's here!"

I shake it all off then look around to realize it was all just a memory of childhood days.

Cynthia Crawford

I first started writing when I was very young. I had a certain knack for putting words together and making sense of my writings. My pre-teen school teachers were amazed by my special gift and developed my skill at writing by giving me topics to write about and recite in class. In junior high, I often wrote for recital in our school auditorium.

Tommy Payne

I believe my PawPaw made little sentences to make conversation. Oh, go on: nobody bothering you. Oh, get you somewhere and sit down. Nobody doing nothing to you. I like to have down time.

William L. Hogan, Jr.

One time when I closed my eyes, my mind went back to my childhood days. I could almost picture my mother's home. I could hear the music playing in the background. It reminded me of when I was at home with my mother. She always had the radio on listening to gospel music. That took me back a few years to when I was young. Then I opened my eyes.

Latasha Jackson

In junior high I had a math teacher and he was different from me. His education and job is the thing that was different than me. He was white and I am black. He was my homeroom teacher and he lived in White Station. He was my math teacher and I was just a student.

William L. Hogan, Jr.

We were one of the first black grammar school baseball teams in the city of Memphis. WDIA radio station along with the Memphis Board of Education sponsored these school baseball teams. Each team belonged to a certain neighborhood as well as the school situated in that particular neighborhood. The rivalry teamwork developing athletic skills was a positive outlet by which we focused our juvenile energies. Those baseball and football teams gave us a positive identity as opposed to street gangs and thuggery, which was also present in our black neighborhoods in the early sixties as well as the present times.

I played shortstop for Mitchell Road Jr. High School. I became very popular for being a left-handed short stop. A position lefties do not usually play because a left-handed shortstop must make a 180 degree pivot to throw a runner out at first. He must be somewhat of a ballet dancer to do this remarkable feat. I had hoped to become the second left-handed shortstop in the major leagues alongside the legendary "Pee Wee" Reese, but as fate would have it, my life took a different direction in my teenage years.

Tommy Payne

Back in the day playing baseball for the radio station for a young black kid was a privilege and a pleasure. My favorite position was shortstop. Now the competition to get the starting position was fierce, but I always managed to win.

You see playing baseball for WDIA was like this, you got to meet the radio personalities and to play at Bellevue Park in the lights at night with the smell of popcorn, peanuts, hot dogs, hamburgers, Bar-B-Que, and fish frying. In our minds we were playing for the New

York Yankees or any one of the Big League teams. Plus all the girls liked and wanted the baseball players and of course we wanted them also.

And then at the end of the game, we helped ourselves to all the concession our little bellies could hold.

Leroy Scott

If I went back to school, I would get to take English and I would like study hall and gym, try to play football, boxing, and basketball. I would sit on the first or second row in seating order. I would buy things for the class and keep them up. I would have them at home and school. I would not smoke and bring things to school that I would work on away from school. I would have a good relation with the teachers and everyone in the school and get me a job and then write about some subjects that I would think to help me in the city. Then I would go home.

William L. Hogan, Jr.

I have dreamed about a reunion with my childhood friend. We decided we would marry loving husbands, have the same amount of children and live across from each other and be best friends forever. I don't know what happened to her. It would be nice to see her again.

I missed my class reunion. I guess the Reunion Committee couldn't locate me. I was in foster care when I graduated and moved after that.

Veyshon Hall

My family never was one to be traditional, other than holiday festivities. I do remember one 4th of July when I was about 7 or 8 years old. My sister, her boyfriend, his friend, his friend's children, and I went downtown on the riverfront for the annual fireworks show. The humidity was surprisingly bearable. The crisp evening breeze smelled of barbecue and something similar to my mommy's fabric softener. All us children rode in the bed of the truck from Nutbush, Tennessee, all the way to the riverfront downtown. I remember the friend backing the truck down the steep gravel hill to park. I was so scared! I knew for sure the truck was gonna fall into the Mississippi! Finally we were settled and started munching on chips and sandwiches. At nightfall, the show began. The loud pops, bangs and booms scared me at first, and I could barely hear anything or anyone. But, in a few minutes, my ears and eyes adjusted and then I saw the beauty of them. The fireworks, lights dancing in the black of the night sky. A smell of sulfur and fish splashing near by. Me and the other kids laid back in the truck bed. Just taking it all in. It felt like the lights were gonna fall down on top of us, or like we could almost reach out and touch them. As the show ended and the mosquitos started to bite we all fell asleep in the back of that truck.

Cynthia Crawford

As a teenager I was a fan of the Jackson Five but my biggest idol was James Brown. James Brown really gave you your money's worth when he put on a show. Some of his earlier records were soul classics. He had a silky smooth voice that was plaintive as well as raunchy and pleading. "Bewildered" was my favorite James Brown record.

Tommy Payne

If I were an athlete, I would be a gymnast. I was always interested in climbing and swinging off of things, especially trees. I liked to play with the different ways I could balance my body, using my hands to go from one end to the other. I love the balance beam and how it allows you to maneuver yourself in an upside down position and walk across it. I would practice for hours a day to make my performance perfect. Being a gymnast requires a lot of healthy eating, so I also like the disciplined diet that it would take to have a gymnast's physique. I also like the way gymnasts are flexible and can do handstands since I would do a lot of handstands and cartwheels when I was younger.

Tamara Hendrix

Baseball is a good sport because every Christmas we would spend at our grandma's and play baseball until I got hit in the nose with the ball. Not too much longer we quit after that. Probably two times after. It wasn't that we go to play ball. The main reason is to be with the family and to eat a Christmas dinner. It's always been a great day at grandma's.

Anthony Johnston

I was fifteen years old when we moved to Memphis. This was the first time I experienced racism.

I remember our car broke down, and my mother had to ride the bus to work at John Gaston Hospital. When she found out that black people had to ride at the back of the bus, she expressed the same indignation as Rosa Parks and wouldn't go to work until our car was fixed. The bus at the Civil Rights Museum always reminds me of my mother in that she risked losing her job rather than ride on the back of a city bus.

Tommy Payne

The family is like blood, more stickier than water, more powerful than Kool-aid. The family means love—togetherness, forgiveness—the power of sharing in the time of one's needs. The family like the one I have, I was raised up in a strict environment. We as a family were given morals and values to live by. Showing respect to other adults or families. The family sometimes are not as close like they should be; because of the personality of each one. I felt like the family should be there for each other; no matter what. There was a time where I left my family because of some shame and guilt; because of what my life had become. I found out that my family just wanted the best of me. It just comes down to that; your family really loves each other. Not just because we come together at funerals or family reunions. The family is love, caring and sharing in the good times or the bad times.

Roderick Baldwin

Years ago when I was about 13 years old I was in the Boy Scouts and on weekends we used to prepare Hobo Stew for the troop. The thing about Hobo Stew is that everyone would bring something to put in the stew, things such as potatoes, tomatoes, celery, onions, bell peppers, corn, beans, peas, greens, squash, okra, eggplant, hot dogs, ground beef, bacon, neck bones, chicken, fish, sausages, steaks, chicken feet, sauce, ham loaf and various spices. There was always some aspiring cooks and troop leaders ready willing and able to prepare the stew and to make cornbread and desserts.

Now, advance about 30 years. I am now preparing food for 250 plus people at Grace-St Luke's Church. After about 4 or 5 trial runs, I find myself having the same pleasure at cooking and watching people eating and enjoying great food. The menu, of course, has grown leaps and bounds from the Hobo Stew days to chicken halves to meat loaf and such. And occasional chili and vegetables and soups and crackers and very tasty desserts. But my cornbread recipe has improved over the years of practice, as well as my uses of spices.

Leroy Scott

LEROY SCOTT

I am Leroy Scott. I was born in Buffalo, New York. I came to Memphis when I was 5 years of age. My family lives in Memphis, New York, Chicago, and Louisiana. The most important event in my childhood was playing baseball for WDIA in the summer at Bellevue Park. The most important event of my adult life was getting married. I'm a grandfather.

I was first without a place to live 10 years ago, when I was 50. I became homeless due to unemployment and illness. I was homeless 3 years. At the time my children were aged 42, 33, and 32. I got into housing 8 years ago. June Averyt told me about the Door of Hope. I began coming to the Writing Group 6 years ago, at the beginning. I was staying at the Door of Hope then. The best thing about writing group is exchanging ideas. The hardest thing is coming up with good subjects. My favorite topic is people. To anyone thinking homeless folks being in a writing group is strange, I'd say, "Come and see for yourself." I'd advise someone thinking of starting a writing group to pay close attention.

I'd like to add that I have enjoyed meeting people at the Door of Hope.

DEDICATION

I would like to dedicate this book to Mrs. June Averyt and my precious children Renea, Ricky and Nicky. For being there for me and about me. I would like to start with my lovely children for they have been my true inspiration and my true reason for living and such a real source of being. And Mrs. June Averyt for being there in my most troubling times in my life. She gave me hope and love when I really needed it. Brought me back from the homeless streets of life and depression when it meant the most to me. And for that I will forever be grateful.

CHAPTER 2
AS WE GREW UP

It was 1969. I was a junior in high school. What I remember the most was my football game against my rival friend Bernard. He was a great fullback that went to Southside High School and I went to Memphis Tech.

It just so happened that I was the school's first black quarterback and I also played safety and punter. Bernard was very fast and deceptive. On that night he scored two touchdowns. I scored one on a 13 yard quarterback keeper. It was very exhilarating. Well we messed around and lost the game but boy did I have fun playing against my buddy Bernard.

Bernard had older brothers so after the game we had a few beers and me and my girlfriend sort of hung out the rest of the evening.

The next day most of the team and I went to Brittling Cafeteria for all you can eat buffet and to a dance. That night that was one of my greatest fall memories.

Leroy Scott

I think the coach of high school was a leader. If you were on his team he would get you some game to play. My father was a leader. He could work as a carpenter and give me some points on the job. My brain with thought is my leader. I hope to go at least 30 more years in my life and if I could keep on depend on this life I would hope, yes, was the answer to live 30 more years.

William L. Hogan, Jr.

Thirty five years ago, there was a young man who started to listen to music on the radio or the albums at home. Listening to the music from the bands hit my ears. The bands I loved was Rare Earth, Fleetwood Mac, Genesis, Lynard Skynard, Journey. There was the Isley Brothers, a non-white group. If it had guitar and drums, that was my speed. I always wanted to play guitar or drums, maybe piano, but couldn't afford the lessons. By the time I was of age, the band Frasier High School said I could be in was a marching band - boy what a trip.

Roderick Baldwin

I remember the hopes and joys of summer after two or three days would fade away. I'm the baby on my mother's side of the family. My sister is 7-1/2 years older than I and was also my live-in babysitter. Whether or not she wanted to be. My mother was mostly a single mom for the majority of my childhood. Always independent and working away from home.

My mom worked 7 a.m. to 7 p.m. most of those years. Which meant she was gone before I woke and didn't return home until it was nearly my bedtime. My summer days consisted of being locked in my mother's bedroom. I would stare out her window. Which wasn't so exciting because the view consisted of a dirt lawn which was maybe 7 to 10 feet wide on the side of the house. That dirt lawn ended at a ditch which partially was filled with trash, debris, and sewer water.

Occasionally, I could get the T.V. to pick up a reception so I could watch "Batman" or "The Beverly Hillbillies." Rarely I could watch "Woody Woodpecker" or "Rocky and Bullwinkle." I had to ask to get out to use the bathroom. My sister also had to cook for me. Lord forbid I learn to do it for myself! Sometimes I would wake up before my sister and go outside to play with some of the neighborhood kids. But when I did I would mostly be locked out of the house until my mom got home. Which means I would then get in trouble for being out after dark!

When I had the privilege of being outside, I now joke that I was practicing for my future experience of homelessness. Which means I mostly used the bathroom outside in the bushes and depended on the kindness of neighbors for food. Otherwise, I missed a lot of meals.

I didn't have many friends or a childhood for that matter. I was never taught how to be a kid. I wasn't happy much unless I was watching T.V. or a movie or I was eating. Because those activities were considered a privilege, not a right.

When I finally learned how to pray, I would repeat, "Dear Lord, let the summer end. Summer, summer, go away and stay there." When the school year started back, I ate more regular meals and had more fun and friends.

Cynthia Crawford

Growing up in a family of eight, under one roof, I learned the necessary steps to keeping it under control and going. Though we had our disagreements, for the most part the ideal of staying in an extended family is to try to make it work; if one of them doesn't try to kill the other! I had the benefit of having each generation (my grandmother being the oldest, then my aunt and uncles, middle-aged, and my cousin, brother, the youngest), so I got a mixture of experiences. I liked hearing about the stories (since my grandmother was raised on a farm) of how my grandmother would have to get up early to feed the chickens, milk the cows, and how it compared to my life, which was opening the refrigerator to get the byproduct of her labor. Family can teach you what values to set for yourself as well as give you the tools to start your own life. Each member has his or her own uniqueness that enriches the others' lives. Family can be challenging to deal with, because of the differences, but in the end you can't pick who you are related to, unless they are married into the family.

Tamara Hendrix

My family is my most cherished possession. I have many cousins. Some in Memphis and some in Louisiana. Most of my aunts and uncles are deceased. They all lived very long and fruitful lives reaching their early 90s. My parents, whom I loved very deeply, did not reach this advanced age. My mother died tragically and my father died less than a year afterwards. They had been married almost 40 years. I have two sisters yet alive and another sister who died from lung disease at 46 years of age. One of my sisters lives in New York City and the other in Dallas, Texas. We communicate often and have very pleasant but sometimes poignant memories of our parents.

I have another family in my wife's relatives. We were next door neighbors, my parents and hers. We started a "serious" relationship at 15 years old. She got pregnant with our oldest daughter in the twelfth grade and we had a basically shotgun wedding so she could graduate from high school. In those times girls who got pregnant in high school were expelled from school. We had two more children and she eventually became a Naval Civil Servant and spent 22 years working in Naval Logistics. She had a massive stroke and has been in a nursing home for the last three years. All her brothers and sisters, nieces, and nephew look upon me as a close family member, and I spend a lot of time with them.

Tommy Payne

For me, graduating high school and then graduating from a two year college was spectacular. I was the first one in my family to finish school and the first college graduate. I was so proud, little did I know animosity was building along the family tree. Family members started treating me differently; I felt like the black sheep of the family. No one wanted to be around me and I couldn't understand why. So my family and I became very distant. There are some who still don't speak to me today. It took many years before anyone finally spoke up and admitted that they were jealous because they didn't have a chance to graduate or attend college. I am reconciled with some family, but the hurt of being pushed away won't ever go away. I now have a great sense of distrust. I love them very much, I just hate all the time that was wasted for nothing.

Veyshon Hall

I was in the ring for the first time in my senior high school days. I was knowing the hook, jab and upper cut. I used that then. I used some punches and then won the fight. I was the coach's best boxer. I got to get in the ring with a champ and I needed work, so I developed me a left side punching system. Just last night I made some attractiveness left side boxing and this will hold the people's attention while I fight good in the ring. I have become actively practicing boxing since the time I had fought in the fairgrounds and won. I never know when that count is given to me that I might be count as a fight. I always do practice moves but since last night I will fight pretty good and always open for fights. William—get into the boxing state with me.

William L. Hogan, Jr.

My greatest day that seems to just stick in my craw is July 1968 football summer practice. We were bused to Memphis Tech High School. Boy, the heat was intense and very dry. We had two practices a day. It was my first time trying out for the Varsity. My position was quarterback (QB), and the QB they had for the past three years was a tall slender white guy named Robert. He was pretty good, and so was I. This made the competition very intense. My edge was that I was a bit faster and I could throw the ball a bit farther. But because Robert was already the starting QB, I had to make as few mistakes as possible.

So as time had it, I picked up some things from Robert and he from me. So with all being that we became somewhat close and friendly. So by the end of summer camp the season started.

Robert was the starter because he started the years before. On some special plays Coach would let me play. I learned quite a bit that year and could hardly wait until next year.

Leroy Scott

I don't know that much about reunions. I have never been to a school, family, relationship reunion. I have been on my own all my life. My mother got killed when I was seven years old. I have not had people in my life that I would want to be reunited with. I would love to have a reunion with my three children one day.

Donna Connie

As the youngest daughter of a single mom who always worked, I was basically raised by my granny. My granny Doris worked 8 hours nearly ever night at the local hospital and babysat me every day while my mommy worked. I remember watching "The Price is Right" with Bob Barker as well as "The Young and the Restless," "General Hospital," and "Another World." I also remember long naps and delicious home cooking. Granny used to stand me up on her footstool next to her at the stove. She would tell me stories of our ancestors and family way back when while teaching me good old family recipes. Life was cooking and cooking was life. You see, cooking in my family isn't about just eating. It's about tastes, sights, sounds, smells, conversations, holidays, arguments, breakups, make-ups, births, deaths, competition, as well as collaboration.

I also went to church with my granny. Sunday school, prayers, and worship was routine. What I remember most about Sunday school was the puppet shows and the rock hard chairs that I always fidgeted in cause they hurt my bottom.

My granny is my inspiration because as a Christian she talked the talk and walked the walk. She loved with all her heart and showed it with her actions. She was my example because she told me how to live and lived it out herself. She could teach me cause she learned a lot of the lessons the hard way. She cared because she knew what it felt like to not be cared for. She helped others because there was a time when others helped her. My love, my heart, my teacher, my listener, my super granny. Dedicated to Doris Ann Cross (Gatlin) born November 3, 1932, home-going July 4, 2004.

Cynthia Crawford

I have adventures of the mind that I take and put to reality. I wanted to play football and I did. It was a time for me and then I wanted to swim and that was a time for me and I boxed and did karate it was a time for me. Sometimes I think up an adventure. I've had many adventures in my lifetime.

William L. Hogan, Jr.

At the age of fifteen, I was chosen to give a dissertation at the old Ellis Auditorium where the Cannon Center now stands. The subject that my high school chose for me was the "religions of the world." This was a subject that I had already read many books about in my early teens. This was also a city wide contest that included all public and private schools.

I earned remarkable grades in high school and was in the top five students that had exceptional I.Q.s. Mine was 155, although I was nowhere near being a genius. My behavior in school was more that of a troubled child than a nerd. I was constantly reprimanded, disciplined, and even suspended from school for fighting and truancy, let alone "collecting" girls. Why I was chosen to represent Hamilton High School had very little to do with my behavior but because of my smarts in spite of being an aggressive teenager.

I studied very hard for this contest. I read more books on religion night and day. Of all the religions I studied, Hinduism won my complete dedication to learn all the aspects of this pantheistic faith. Yoga became more a religion than a system of exercising the body. So I bought books on the practice and began doing yoga positions at about 16 years old.

Tommy Payne

My first time I experienced drugs was at 16 years old. It was marijuana in a joint. When I finished school that year in 1985, I enrolled in college at Baker Junior College. I was studying to become a (RN) Nurse. That summer went by and I got a phone call from a friend that I used to work with at General Motors. So that year on January of 1986 I was hired at 19 years old and was making 16.00 dollars a hour. Time passed and I began to work 2nd shift, which led to me dropping out of college to work. During that time, I was hanging out with an older crowd of people and I started to drink, smoke pot, and go out to clubs until morning. My life was about to spin from under me and I was hard-headed and too foolish to see what was going to happen to me down the road. I wouldn't go to church, but God had his way of getting my attention, but I wouldn't listen because I wanted the worldly lifestyle, being a single woman with the freedom to do the wrong things in my life.

Robbin K

One day I was walking down the street and it was hot as an 8 hour range, and I noticed an old man under a shade tree drinking a beer. Now doctors say that is not good to drink alcohol beverages in the heat but you couldn't tell by the way he was drinking that beer. So I said I must have one. So I got me a beer and started drinking it. At first it was great then I started to get hot and sluggish. I believe my blood pressure went up and I started to feeling sick so I went inside to get me some air conditioning and an aspirin and started feeling somewhat better. So from that day on I learned a valuable lesson – don't drink on a hot day outside. I believe that hot weather and alcohol does not mix and that hot weather and a cool water is a great mix.

Leroy Scott

I was born in Memphis and finished high school at Melrose in Orange Mound. I went to Memphis Area Vocational Technical School. I have 2 girls and 2 boys by Donald Perry Phillips. I worked at the Memphis City Schools. I worked in warehouses. But today I have a lawyer and waiting on a hearing for Social Security.

Jacqueline Crowder

I enlisted into the United States Navy. I had to go in under the delayed entry program due to my age. So I had the whole summer to work. I had to wait for my next birthday, also my parents had to consent, which they signed the papers for me. Because I wanted to see the world. I served six years. I went to boot camp in Orlando, Florida. I did my "A" school in Millington, TN and I was stationed at Sigonella, Sicily.

WJS

I was very fortunate to have actually met Elvis when I was younger and in High School. I was working at a hotel apartment. My boss was from Scotland and he would tell me stories about Scotland and his boyhood years. In the hotel was a lounge downstairs called the Thunderbird Lounge where all the cool cats hung out, and it came to be that Elvis would be the most famous. I would wait on Elvis and his entourage and they would leave pretty big tips. One thing that would really stick out in my mind is how sharp he was and Priscilla. The leather suits, diamond rings and how gracious they would be.

I remember one time on a Sunday night. People in Memphis had a thing about looking at Cadillacs at Madison Cadillacs and this nurse was looking at a pretty Cadillac, and Elvis walked up to her and asked her did she like Cadillacs and she said yes so he told her to pick one. She picked a white one and he said that one was his and to pick another one and he would buy it for her the next day and he did. And it came to be one of his regular things he did for people.

Leroy Scott

Snowflakes flitter flutter
from heaven to the earth.
Chilling to the touch, yet
beautiful to the eye.
Drifting, floating in time
and space.
Sparkling when the light hits
them just right.
Snowflakes no two are alike.
Each and everyone delicately
crafted by GOD's own hands.
When clumped together in a
bowl sprinkled with sugar and
lemon juice, how sweet a treat.
And when millions fall over the land how beautiful the
covered trees, bushes, and ground.
Just beware of the yellow
snow!

Cynthia Crawford

As a youngster I was always a cut up in grammar school. The principal's office was my home room. I was good at playing practical jokes on the other kids in my neighborhood. I loved to fight and knock chips off other boys' shoulders.

At about sixteen, I was diagnosed as being bipolar.

My fun loving ways became sullen depression. I quit going to school and began acting sort of mean spirited. All my friends thought I was just playing some kind of mean joke and would go back to my old, devious, funny ways.

But the joke was on me this time. I had a very serious, suicidal, mental disorder. But everyone thought I was just the boy crying wolf. Now, a real wolf had taken over my personality. And for the rest of my life I would be dependent on anti-depressant drugs. The boy who cried wolf to scare his friends and laugh about it had been eaten by a real wolf. But everyone thought I was playing another one of my mischievous games.

Tommy Payne

JOCKLUSS THOMAS PAYNE

I am Thomas Payne. I was born in Lake Charles, Louisiana. The most important event of my childhood was moving to Memphis when I was 14 years old. My family lives in Memphis and Louisiana. The most important event of my adult life has been getting off drugs. I am a grandfather and a great-grandfather.

The first time I was without a place to live I was 47 years old. I was homeless for 2 years. I became homeless again for a year. I was divorced while I was homeless. I had adult children. I got into housing in 2006. I heard about the Door of Hope while working at the Union Mission. I began coming to writing group in 2007. I was then staying at the Door of Hope. I kept coming to writing group because it gives me a chance to express my feelings constructively. What I most enjoy about writing group is meeting people and hearing their stories. There is nothing hard about writing group. My favorite topic is politics. To those who think homeless folks in a writing group is strange, I'd invite them to come join us. If you are thinking of starting a writing group, I'd advise you to be honest. I hope our book will be successful.

DEDICATION

I would like to dedicate this book to Marilyn "Kat," my first and only wife. Kat has been my constant companion for over 47 years. We started out as teenage sweethearts and became the parents of three children. One is dead. Miss Kat, as she is known, is a very sweet woman. She has an outgoing smile and disposition, making friends with just about anyone on first impression.

She is a humanistic person. Very lovable and motherly. She mothered me for most of my life. Treated me like a wayward child. She was always there when I needed her. She still gives me a knowing smile. Even though she has been in a nursing home for 11 years now, she has been an inspiration towards my independence from alcohol and drugs.

She has met my present companion and they hit it off nicely. Miss Kat is the love of my life. For life or death we will always remain together.

CHAPTER 3
WHEN WE BECAME ADULTS

I developed major depression and certain mental disorders that compromised my talent for writing. I never really lost the ability to write but my writings became inflammatory and racially motivated. This seems like centuries ago, not just a few decades past.
Tommy Payne

Coming from a very quiet rural setting in Mississippi as a little boy, coming to a big city was like a fairy tale of seeing all the lights and tall buildings of businesses and shops. It was very exciting. And the big thing is the River—after reading and hearing all the stories of Old Man River—the history—cotton and trades—the slave market. I had never as a boy seen a river or seen a city until I came to Memphis. The musical heritage environment was so interesting. I still go to downtown and the River, and remember what happened and what it looked like years ago and how people lived back in time. The way the system was—the struggles all mankind went through. Memphis has a lot of history to tell, I wanted to know it. Beale Street, the stories of gambling, pawn shops, retail, music, bars—when whites were only down on Beale but once or twice a week there. I found out there was a lot of mansions in the downtown area. People coming from travel off the River. The very interesting thing about the history of Memphis; it is a beautiful city and growing. The River and the city is changing every day. I want to be part of change.
Roderick Baldwin

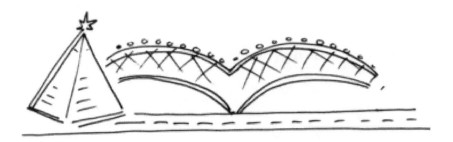

My earliest memory of Memphis was when I came to visit Memphis in 2009. I took a ride on the trolley. It was exciting to take a tour around downtown Memphis. It's really interesting to see the unique sights and sounds of downtown. I liked riding around on the train making stops at interesting places like the Civil Rights Museum and Beale Street. I like seeing vendors selling their goods at the park. I love riding by, smelling hot dogs, onions and bell peppers cooking on the grill. My favorite part was seeing the old Mississippi River.

Latasha Jackson

I was stationed in Sicily. It's a small island at the bottom of Italy. Even though they are close to each other, they don't belong to each other. Like West Memphis, Arkansas is to Memphis, TN.

When Christmas arrived, I was asleep. I woke early, went and had breakfast. I didn't have to cook for we ate free at the Mess Hall. I went into town with some friends because we were missing our families. So we sight-seen the towns of Messina, Costa Saracena and Taromina. The Mediterranean Sea Coastline of Taromina I enjoyed the most that day. A deep blue-green aqua coloring and the further out a darker blue ocean. It was beautiful. We made it back to Base so we could have a traditional dinner, and went clubbing at the USO.

WJS

I remember back in the '70s when we were wearing platform shoes and bellbottom pants with tight long sleeve shirts. I had a pair of platform shoes with goldfish in the soles and heels with water and greenery. They used to look really good in the day time in the sun. It was a wild fad that all of the brothers were going through all over the nation. The thing was to see who could be the most extravagant and colorful, in other words who could be the most fly. The movie Superfly, a movie by Gordon Parks Jr., was very impressioned on the scene, as well as Shaft and Cotton Come to Harlem as well as a host of others. The only thing about the shoes that can be short lived is that you couldn't run in them without them breaking or you breaking your neck.

Leroy Scott

I got into Bruce Lee in 1973 the year of his Death. I met Chuck Norris the man he fought in Return of the Dragon at Bill Wallace Karate School learn today's Karate. His emotion, Bruce did emotion and feeling in his face along with his fighting things you could not catch in your mind and so he made it good and real.

About Bruce Lee, he's like god. You never supposed to forget the like of him. Remember Bruce is a part of you.

William L. Hogan, Jr.

"1, 2, 3, 4, 5, 6, 7, 8, 9, 10, let it out. Take a deep breath and PUSH! 1...2...3...4...5...6...7... hold it in 8...9... you can do it, PUSH...10. Let it out," says the nurse. "Man, Lord help me!" I scream sweat pouring, mouth so dry I can taste cotton. Lips also dry and chapped. My mom feeling empathy for me and not having any Chapstick decides to put some of her pinkish red lipstick on my lips, for moisture I believe. At this point in labor and delivery I've been laboring for nearly 44 hours and pushing for one and a half hours! "What's wrong?" my mom asks the doctor. (Apparently, there was a lip the baby just couldn't get over and past. I still to this day don't understand exactly what they meant.) Despite having an epidural in my tailbone, my back and bottom feel like they're on fire with pain and cramps. My head is pounding, and I haven't eaten in over 24 hours.

With a crackle a lady's voice comes over the PA system, "The patient's sister is here. Can she come in?" My grandmother has been here for probably 6 or 7 hours at this point. So being her sweet gracious self she chooses to leave so my sister can come in. I'm still pushing as she enters through the door. In the 10 seconds that it takes her to cross the room and step up to the bed, out pops a pink wrinkled 7 pound 9-1/2 ounce bundle of love and joy. Next thing I know, my mother appears to be in a trance. Every move the doctor and nurses make while holding, cleaning, or swaddling my newborn girl, Mother is on their heels. Not once does she take her eyes off my newborn. Suddenly I feel something wet dripping on and down my head and face. Looking up, I'm engulfed in the arms of my sister leaning down and embracing me. Her tears of joy and mine mingle together on the bed.

All the division that has occurred in my family over the past few months seems to evaporate with those tears.

Cynthia Crawford.

I know in my family it was the upmost importance that the child get out and make a life of its own. Some do take a while to develop to being independent and not leaning on the mother or father to carry them. I grew up in a strict household. It was about having or making something of yourself. You have to pay your way somehow, even if it is just cleaning or keeping the house in order. There was a time where I needed to come back home - until I got my act together.

Roderick Baldwin

Back in the early '70s I was involved in a lot of traffic wrecks and was involved in a lot of lawsuits. So one day it all came to a head and I collected $25,000. I was blown away. I bought a brand new car of my choice that I always wanted and several other things.

The best gift that I gave was $2000 to my mother and $1000 to my three sisters. It really made me feel good to see the smiles on their faces and the hugs and kisses that followed.

Leroy Scott

My parents were members of the NAACP as well as the Student Nonviolent Coordinating Committee. An organization Dr. King founded in Atlanta. Firstly composed of African Exchange Students and later Afro-American freedom fighters as well. But peaceful. I didn't agree with nonviolence. I held a clinched fist up high in the air and shouted Alla U Ackbar! Our freedom must be won by bloodshed. In the name of God.

The followers of Dr. King would not join with us. Peaceful non-violence was a worn record to me. They persisted with nonviolence. We were tired of lynchings, beatings, fire-hosings, police dogs, and dingy jails. We would fight back. Dr. King meant well but we couldn't see that. To us he was a cowardly Uncle Tom depending on the good graces of the white folks.

But immediately after his death the nation was reeled and rocked by spontaneous violence, beatings, burnings, killings. For the first time in history white people were scared of us. Nine members of the black panthers were lined up in a street in Chicago and shot down in cold blood by the FBI. It didn't change a thing. Symbionese Liberation Army members stormed a courtroom and shotgunned a white judge to death and two bailiffs.

I am finally able to see Dr. King for the man he was and I will treasure his memory for the rest of my life. Now, I am at last a peaceful citizen. He was right and I was wrong.

Tommy Payne

My first real job was when I graduated from vocational school back in 1971. My new job was a welder at International Harvester. It was truly amazing and wonderful. Finally I was able to get some of the things that I wanted like a new car, condominium, furniture, stereos, TVs and plenty of clothes and shoes. I was able to start a family and have children. I was very blessed to have had a job that I truly wanted and loved, a very big and famous plant world wide making farm equipment such as cotton pickers, hay balers, combines, disc harrow and various tractor and truck parts. I must have welded at least 2000 or more different parts over a 15 year period, from cotton picker axles to trailer bars.

Leroy Scott

At a very early age I learned that if you want something you have to work for it. That included an education, clothes, shoes, food, etc. I made up my mind then to always have a job because money is a necessity. My first job was a Penny Saver route. I worked hard at that job and every one after that. Most of my employers said the same thing about my performance: You're an excellent worker and responsible, but you need to work on your attitude.

My response was always, "Yes Sir/Madam." In my mind though, I'm saying Yeah, well if my co-workers actually worked maybe I wouldn't be so angry myself.

Veyshon Hall

The afternoon sitting there with a concerned look on my face! A normal sunny day. She comes into the front room—slow and quiet! I speak but the return is slow! Her light walk lets me know what she has been through! Here it is 9 years later, I go through the same thing and pray that God helps me and keeps me.

Roderick Baldwin

I went to a Midtown mental health a long time ago and I ran into a nice woman We talked about things that we were doing something with a book. So I went to her one day and I asked to write a small book about my muscles and I also mentioned writing a tall book. I met a great doctor who healed my wounds that I got from riding a motorcycle. He healed me and that was someone who was great to me.

William L. Hogan, Jr.

In my Journey of Life I have met and connected with many types of people. One of the most interesting people that I met was a man where I was working. I was a welder and he worked on the cotton picker line on the second shift. One night he needed a ride to get something to eat. So we left and he wanted to go to the liquor store. I said ok but at that time I wasn't drinking alcohol so I took him and he went and brought two half pints of vodka and I went to Tops Bar B. Q. for a sandwich and a coke. So on the way back he threw one of the half pints away. I said you mean you drank that half pint already. He said yes and that he was going to take the other one in the building for break. I was truly amazed that a person could drink like that so I wondered what was going on. Come to find out that he had a break up with his girlfriend and he took it real hard and people thought he was just a drunk.

But come to find he was a master chef, brick layer and real sharp dresser, very well versed in music, polite and a host of other things that would amaze you.

Leroy Scott

I have traveled to Mississippi and Michigan and flew on an airplane to Paris Island South Carolina and I have went on short Memphis Travel places. I think it takes a lot of money to do travel. I have a lot of experiences on my travel. I got to see a lot of new places on the time I traveled. It took a lot of time for me to see it all but it was good and I learned a lot.

William L. Hogan, Jr.

I would like to talk about a time I experienced crime in Memphis first hand. It was about thirty years ago, a friend and I was at a pool hall on the infamous Dunlap and Mosby St. We were playing a game of pool and talking trash when four guys came in with shotguns and shot up in the ceiling and said everyone get the freaking money out of your pockets right now, let's not make this a murder. Just a robbery and of course we did as they asked.

When it was over I must have shook for a week thinking about what could have happened.

Thank God no one was hurt, and I never went back in there asking for anything.

Leroy Scott

While stationed in Sicily, I was raped. Someone had spiked my drink (orange juice) with liquid quaaludes. I was also pregnant at the time. I had my first child at the age of 20. She was born in Naples, Italy. With me being in the military, that gave her the status of dual citizenship. In February 1982 I was stationed in Kingsville, Texas. While there I met my husband.

WJS

I was once married.

Absence makes the heart grow fonder. And old adage that I feel so well. The greatest absence in my life is that of my parents. My mother died when I was 33 years old and my father soon followed her in about a year or so.

They were humble people who gave me a lot of good ol' country common sense. The chewing tobacco kind of old fashioned common sense. Yes, my mother chewed tobacco and dipped snuff at the same time. How she never swallowed the juices always amazed me.

I miss their country ways. We often went fishing together and they got jealous because I always caught more fish than they did. My mother talked incessantly and spit tobacco juice in the lake. She actually scared the fish away. She just couldn't understand that fish could hear.

My father was very soft spoken and friendly. He would do just about anything my mother told him to do. Their love for each other always filled me with a sense of belonging to a blessed family.

They were always there for me when I needed them. Regardless to whatever I needed them for. Many times I needed them to make bonds for me and hire lawyers. They never questioned me or refused me. They only prayed for me. Their absence from my life taught me really what the real world was like. When they passed away I felt hopeless and totally alone. But they instilled in me the roots of being a man. I had to go on and do what I needed to do in order to survive the real world.

Their absence was also a blessing. For once I had to stand on my own two feet and - be a man.

I still miss them even though it's been 30 some years since their deaths.

Tommy Payne

The people I met in the past I can remember well, but time has passed by and I only see a vision. They are absence from my life. I had a good time with them. I remember all the things these people did for me and now I can't remember their face and I like those people but the time of change made me forget them. I would like to sit and think about many of them. All I remember of them now is the re-membrance of them is lost. Well I must go on now. The people of today is what I am keeping up with now. I have a lot of things in my mind today and I can remember most of what I am doing today. I am thankful for what I have today.

William L. Hogan, Jr.

I was in Houston TX at the gulf coast fishing at night. The lights on the water, standing in the water, feeling the tide come in on my white tennis shoes and making them wet.

The great smell of the night air and the fish. Cigars and beer.

Swimming in it, and the taste of salt and sand.

The slapping of the water against the pier and my legs and the roaring of the gulf itself.

It felt refreshing and somewhat gritty because of the sand.

It was a feeling of freedom and good cheer late night fishing and drinking with my best friends and enjoying the time with them.

Leroy Scott

I have worked as a gas station attendant, medical secretary, house cleaner, home health aide, warehouse worker, sales person, daycare provider, CNA, cook, data entry clerk and a legal secretary. Talk about multi-talented. All that hard work and experience did not prepare me for unemployment or homelessness.

Veyshon Hall

Leaving my home in New York to find someone to sell my music—this was hard at first. I was not lucky. It took years and I got into trouble along the way. Within six to seven years ago before I arrived in Memphis. I met a man from Atlantic Records and he signed me up twice. I was ready and leaving home and looking forward to being able to return with a new career in the art of selling songs and singing. Going home now would be nice just to be able to tell about my time away from New York.

Master Major Joshua Williams

MASTER MAJOR JOSHUA WILLIAMS

I am Master Major Joshua Williams. I was born in Manhattan, New York. The most important event of my childhood was going to school and being in New York. I've got family in New York, Memphis and Louisiana. The most important event of my adult life is my family and the children. I came to Memphis in 2006, which was the first time I was without a place to live. I became stranded in Memphis. I was homeless one year. I heard about the Door of Hope from June Averyt and another at Door of Hope. I was staying at the Door of Hope in 2007 when I started coming to writing group. I kept coming to writing group because of the topics and what is on my mind. I most enjoy the way Miss Ellen gives the topic. My favorite topic is writing about the homeless. The hardest thing is when people laugh out in group. If someone thought homeless folks in a writing group was strange,

I'd say that care and kindness is the way to look at homeless people. I'd advise others starting a writing group to take their time and think things through—not everybody is going to hear you. I'd like for folks to know that the Door of Hope is a nice place and gives people a place to stay—it's got good rules everywhere.

DEDICATION

I want to dedicate this book to my family. Payne Williams Wang Wong and to Mr. and Mrs. Stafford family and friends. The reason why is cause they are there for me and welcome me with prayers. I say it over and over, they open doors for me when I'm working and when I'm not working. They show the love and they share true values too. Being homeless, I'm glad someone shares. To give to a human being is believing in that person. You can get on your feet and you can work and be a working part of your human race. People give pride and hope that lift heads.

Master Major Joshua Williams

PART II
OUR LIVES DURING HOMELESSNESS

CHAPTER 4
WHAT SENT US INTO HOMELESSNESS

Homeless! I can't believe this happened to me. Lord I don't understand. I paid the rent, and still I came home from work to find my belongings sitting in the yard. Oh! The humiliation! The shame, the pain. I hated having people passing by and laughing. I guess they thought it was funny. I wonder how they would feel if it was them. I went to a homeless shelter. They made me leave when my money got funny (whoever heard of paying rent to stay at a shelter). I'm slowly but surely working my way back up though. Being homeless brought an awful change to my life. I pray to God please help me to get a house soon.

Latasha Jackson

What really burns my butt about homelessness is that everyone thinks that we are all drug addicts and that's simply not the case all the time. I personally know quite a few people that's homeless and not on drugs. I used to feel sorry for people that looked down on homeless people until I put it in the Lord's hands because what they don't know is that the very ones they are looking down on are the very ones they are going to need when and if they become homeless.

So in closing, let me be the first to say this: don't be so fast to judge. Live and let live.

Leroy Scott

So I continued to work at various jobs until the day the doctor said you cannot go back to work, you're killing yourself. Whatever, that doctor doesn't know anything. I have bills to pay so it's off to work I go.

Beep, beep, beep. These are the sounds I hear when I wake up in the hospital after my third stroke. I guess the doctor knew more than I thought. I haven't ever known what not working was. It is difficult to be doing, then all of a sudden be not able to do. Guess that's the true meaning of disabled.

Veyshon Hall

My world started to spin out of control. I was working another job as secretary and I started a relationship with a man who would use drugs too. I started to get high daily. I snorted cocaine, took pills and drank liquor and beer. All I wanted to do is stay high everyday, because I lost my sight of things in life. I had very low self-esteem about myself. I just stopped loving myself as a person. I know God still had his hands on my life, but I fell deeper and deeper into worldly things.

Robbin K

I knew that going home would be a trip but I had to try. So in spite of all odds I set out to get busy. Going home to me was a loser's way and I always wanted to win. Looking back I wondered how many times am I going to start over. Well I was determined that this was it. I got home and about 10 minutes in I saw the difference. I am the only son so that meant that on Thanksgiving Day I made the menu for dinner for the family—I called mother and got her ready to go to the store to shop for the dinner. I called her to let her know I was on my way. So when I got there there was no answer to my amazement because she was so prompt. So I knocked harder and still no answer. So I took the spare key and went in and called out to her and still no answer. I went through the house and found her laying on the bathroom floor in her blood and panicked. So I grab her in my arms and try to revive her. It did no good. I call 911. They came and pronounced her dead. Also that was my 30th birthday. I was totally broken hearted but strangely I saw a new light and felt better as if God was telling me that everything was going to be alright.

About 10 years later the plant that I worked at closed. I was going job-to-job to keep living. Then I had one of my three heart attacks. And then a few years later I had an aneurism and went on disability. My disability was long and slow coming so I became homeless. Because the reason was that I could no longer work and had no income to pay rent and was eventually evicted from my apartment. After a couple of years of homelessness I got with the Door of Hope and was able to reflect on my life and family. It was very touch and go. When my disability finally came I was able to see my family a lot more. So the revelation was great and I thank the lord for being real again.

Leroy Scott

My husband was wonderful then, attentive, sensitive, kind, respectful, all you want out of a husband. We had our first child in June 1983, while in Texas. June is also our anniversary month. He got out of the military in 1984. And found a job. I didn't get out until a year later, November of 1985. We moved to Colorado and made that our home.

WJS

My story is not for the faint of heart. Two hearts meet, shared a love neither could explain or understand. Then less and less time shared together drove a wedge between the two. Sure enough comes the ultimate betrayal, like a Harlequin Romance. The two forced to part, and make a new start. The ill fated beauty, with no support from family or friend lost everything. But gained so much more.

Cynthia Crawford

D edicated
O rdained
O bedient
R eapers

O beying the
F ather

H onest
O rderly
P eace, that's
E verlasting

When my time was up at the rehab, I had nowhere to go and no money. One day I went to eat lunch at the Door of Hope. I didn't know anything about the help they offered. One of the staff was kind enough to ask me why I looked sad. I told her my story and the rest is a success story. They helped me find a nice place and paid my rent, too. Soon I was able to pay the whole rent, everyone was proud, especially me. All because of God's love flowing through the employees, volunteers, clients and donors. Door of Hope saved me from hardship and loved me back to a productive member of society. Thank you all!! Two years plus later I am still a proud client of Door of Hope . . .

To be continued
Veyshon Hall

VEYSHON HALL

I am Veyshon Hall. I was born in West Memphis, Arkansas. I came to Memphis in 2000. My family lives in New York, Memphis, Arkansas, Florida, and Germany. The most important event in my adult life has been getting a pacemaker inserted. I'm a grandmother.

I was first without a place to live in 1987 when I was 22 years old and had a newborn. I became homeless because of drug use. I was homeless one year. I became homeless again in 2010 when my children were 23 and 19. I am still homeless. I heard about the Door of Hope in drug rehab. I began coming to writing group in 2010 when I was still in rehab. I kept coming to writing group because I started writing and also to connect with other people. What I enjoy most is getting to express myself. The hardest thing is transportation to group. My favorite topic is anything funny.

To those who think homeless folks in a writing group is strange, I'd say, "I think you're strange too." To others thinking of starting a writing group, I'd say, "Keep writing alive." Thank you to the Door of Hope for allowing me to be a part of the writing group. Thank you Mrs. Ellen for teaching/leading/loving us. Thank you.

DEDICATION

I dedicate this with Love to Antwaun who grew up strong in spite of me. To Christine, who has been more of a parent to me than I have to her. To my lovebirds, whose love is unconditional. To Ellen who is the best teacher. The Door of Hope for letting me be me (whew) thank you. To God, for his Grace and Mercy and continuous Love. To the writers group and writers everywhere. Keep being yourself, keep writing and pray, pray, pray. And finally to myself for not giving up.

CHAPTER 5
DAY-TO-DAY WITHOUT A HOME

The rent has to be paid; I don't have it.
I'm sick and unable to work; what to do?
I asked around for help from different agencies.
I'm getting depressed and worrying like crazy.
Then I did what I needed to do: I prayed.
You wouldn't believe what God said.
"Come. No line! No waiting!"
                                        Veyshon Hall

Last year I was busy in my own house, and finishing raising my children. I had a job, and I got paid every week. I looked forward to going shopping every weekend, after I paid the bills. Me and my family would go to our favorite restaurant every week. Now since I lost my job everything has changed. I'm not going shopping every week any more. I'm also not going to my favorite restaurant any more. My children have grown up and are on their own. I have also moved from my house. I'm now in the process of getting a smaller place. I love my children, but I'm going to enjoy living by myself.
                                        Latasha Jackson

Being on the street, I had no contact with my son or my immediate family. They had no idea where I was. My mind would constantly think of him, but I couldn't get myself to call. I felt like such a failure, so I didn't want to call. But when I got myself together and made up my mind that was not fair to my family, God provided people and scenarios where my family could find me. Although I miss them, I don't regret the decision to place my son with his father, so that he could have a stable life.

Tamara Hendrix

Homelessness is not fun, not to me anyway. Day by day, I wandered at night. I try finding places to sleep. There's a lot of them thinks that it doesn't matter, that it's a game you play but it's not. Because I wonder where to sleep and eat but I found places to eat a lot easier than to sleep.

Anthony Johnston

There was a time being homeless when I would have to plan out my day—by going to a church to get in the soup line for a meal for that day. I remember going through the fear of talking to certain people to find out where the other outlets was to get vouchers for food or to find a place to lay my head. There was a time one night I had nowhere else to go; I slept in Court Square under the pavilion. I really didn't know too much about the mission or how to get in there, but I followed the lead of some guys I befriended. Because of the extra things we were doing; it really helped! There were so many times that I can share with you. But the main thing was to survive the street and the elements. I am thankful for God giving me the Spirit to do something about my problem of homelessness, or I could walk around and complain about what people wasn't giving me. But use the resources to help get out of homelessness and not asking for handouts—asking the system the right way.

Roderick Baldwin

When I first started using drugs I had the ability to seem normal and carry on like ordinary people. Even while under the influence of drugs.

Years passed and drugs—plus alcohol use—began to take its toll. I could no longer hold decent jobs or function creatively. I even drifted into homelessness, along with my wife. Both our lives became unmanageable. We lost houses, furniture, cars, and even self respect. Drug use became a daily ritual while we drifted farther and farther into ghetoism.

Tommy Payne

My reason for writing this is because it was a concern very deep in my heart. A friend indeed was very special to me because it was in a way about race relation and to me being from New York and now settling in the Dirty South meant a lot. It was this very nice white lady opening up her heart and influences to me at a time when it seemed no one else would, even people I have known for years.

Leroy Scott

So I moved to Portland, OR at 20 years old to move in with my brother in his studio apartment. I moved to Portland to run from my addiction. I got a job at a hotel in downtown Portland as a housekeeper. I worked as a housekeeper for 8 months until one day after work I had the urge to get high so I found a person and he told me where I could go to get high and get drugs. I was off again getting high and lost my job. I did not want to tell my brothers that I started to get high and decided to hit the streets causing me to be homeless for 6 months. I slept under bridges and on park benches because I wanted to get high. One day I found myself on the streets selling my body to get high. I just wanted the drugs and wanted to stay high, so I wouldn't have to face my life's reality.

Robbin K

My best memory was waking up every day and going to eat at the radio station soup kitchen. I liked the time of waking up and going. One goal I have is to get up and go walking. It is one of the best things for me. I love to walk.

William L. Hogan, Jr.

New Beginnings… Today is a good day! Over the past year I have seen God work many miracles in my life. I am able to truly appreciate all of them. There was a time in my life when that was not the case. I took and took anything and everything I could. I was arrogant and felt like life owed me something. Boy, was I so, so WRONG! I remember the first time I became homeless in 2001. I was still young. A mere 19 years old. Even at that point in life, throughout it all I never learned my lesson. Until in 2009 I ended up homeless a second time. I cried every chance I got a moment alone. I also remember 5 fearful nights sleeping alone in my truck which I had parked in a very secluded and dark parking lot. For the most part they were sleepless and restless nights. I was literally so scared something would happen that I had the shakes. I occasionally dozed off for a few minutes here and there. But until I got into the Salvation Army Women's Lodge (on December 19th, 2009), I didn't get a full night's sleep. I remember changing and washing up in public restrooms like McDonald's or the library. None of my friends or family knew what was going on.

Once I ended up in the shelter, some friends and family said, "I didn't know! You should have said something! I would have helped you!"

A year and a half later I was truckless and homeless a third time. My friends and family weren't there anymore. I found my way to the church where I had grown up with my granny. I attended that night's service. As people started to leave, my heart sank and I realized I had nowhere to go. I swallowed my shame and asked the pastor if I could sleep in one of the Sunday School classrooms. On the couch. He said no because the security system was so powerful any movement would set it off. So I walked to the grocery store next door. I walked around just looking. When the store closed, I walked back to the church and sat on the front steps and said a prayer for God's protection. Then I proceeded to walk around the church building until I found a soft grassy spot in a corner of the outside of the building where I slept two nights in a row. Through a friend I got connected to a caseworker in Frayser. I got a referral to Door of Hope. Within 6 months I was blessed with a rental home. It was furnished by Door of Hope.

Today I am in the process of moving into a 3-bedroom apartment in Whitehaven which will afford me the opportunity to reunite with my children.

I am not writing this for your sympathy or to get anything from you. I write this to let you know I'm still human. And if you are currently experiencing homelessness, hopefully this will be a ray of sunshine to not give up. This WILL NOT last forever. YOU CAN get through this! YOU ARE WORTH IT! ANYTHING that's WORTH IT takes a little pain and hard work. In the end you will be STRONGER and BETTER!

Cynthia Crawford

Living in boarding homes I always thought wasn't good but what I found in boarding homes is good people, good staff, and good food. But I still would like to have a house I can call my own. Living in a rooming home is the same as a boarding home. Good people, good staff, and good food. This is my story.

Anthony Johnston

Freedom is being able to come and go as you please and having peace of mind. I don't have my freedom right now. I'll be so glad when I can have my freedom. I have to be in at a certain time. Some people try to take all your money. Oh how I long for my freedom. Sometimes I feel like a prisoner. My freedom is very limited right now. I'm waiting to get my own place again. I really hate having to live in someone else's place. You have to eat what they say. People treat you like crap. When you go through a crisis and have to live with them, you are living in prison, and they are the prison warden. I hate having to live under someone else's rules. Freedom to me is having my own place. I will be so glad when I can be free again.

Latasha Jackson

Friends are a silver fines.
Sand senses is a silver must gold.
You have a day/dreams of mink and silver & gold.
The bond of right – true is – in the silver water sand gold.
The Dream ends, not the sand
or the silver – gold.

Master Major Joshua Williams

When I was homeless and did not have a place to stay, a friend asked me to come and stay for a couple of days. I enjoyed staying there. I got a chance to take a shower, change clothes, comb my hair and eat dinner and also wash the dirty clothes that I had on. I enjoyed getting a good night sleep. What a friend I had. Thank you Jesus for answering my prayers.

Jacqueline Crowder

I came across a man who took me over to his house and I didn't realize he had 10 locks on the back door. So I started to proceed in the bedroom and I sat on his bed. He told me the money was under his bed. First a voice inside told me not to go, but I didn't listen because I wanted the drugs. He pulled a machete knife and hit my coat. I jumped up and ran to the back door. I saw the locks on the door so I asked Jesus "Please Save Me Lord." I heard a big boom and all the locks were open, so I ran out and proceeded to run for my life. This was one of His miracles Jesus showed me in my life. The things I endured out there – Jesus's precious blood saved me, because I had a purpose in this life.

Robbin K

Homelessness is a struggle to survive on a daily basis. You have to eat to have energy enough to maintain the struggle. So your first stop is at a soup kitchen to get a cup of soup and a bologna sandwich. Sometimes a doughnut or crackers.

Food is a basic need. It occupies a great part of your time. Time that could probably be used to find some kind of employment. But you can't work hungry. It's a devastating cycle. You dread the sunrise because it represents another day of aimlessness. Going from soup kitchen to soup kitchen. You dread the sunset because it represents another night of fighting the cold or biting mosquitoes. Usually in some abandoned building or house. It's depressing and frustrating. You're in the limbo of a fruitless life style. You become hostile or you can become weak and be stepped upon by a volatile society.

Tommy Payne

When my rent was due, I went to the Door of Hope for help. They welcomed me with open arms and did all humanly possible to help me. I trusted without question and didn't worry. Not only were they helping with the rent, they were gonna help me get a voucher for an apartment. Was I happy and grateful? Without question. So I moved to transitional housing (a shelter). Hey, it was for only 30 days, so I couldn't go wrong. I felt bad for the other women in the transitional home who were truly homeless with nowhere to go. Little did I know that they were better off than I.

After being convinced and finally believing I was going to get a housing voucher, I was told I was not eligible. Wow! The bottom fell out of my world. I am truly homeless with nowhere else to go. As the other women moved out into their apartments, I became angrier and depressed. I cried and cried and I still cry sometimes now. I'm still angry, depressed and sad, yet I still have faith in the Door of Hope. Only now, my faith in God comes first!

It's okay to depend on others, just don't make them your God. Thanks, Door of Hope. Praise God!

To be continued …

Veshon Hall

It's an awful thing to live in turmoil. Sometimes in order to get peace I think you have to get to know God. Sometimes you have to resolve some of your issues. Sometimes you have to let go of something. Sometimes you have to get hold to something. I believe you can find peace in a trying situation. If you trust in God, I believe he will give you peace.

Latasha Jackson

I was living at the Salvation Army and a girl who lived there decided to throw all the women a pizza party. The night before the pizza party I had a dream. I dreamed that all the women at the Salvation Army were in a white AA meeting van going home and the girl who was throwing the party saw her husband and left with him. I screamed, what about our pizza party. What a weird dream. But the pizza party was great.

Donna Connie

I had a case manager who I told I needed some ID
and a guy took me to a place selling ID
for eight dollars
and I had purchased a ID with my picture
all of my size of the collar was showing.
I'm always of time with my face the picture and collar.

Oh how I wish I have tall spaces in my forearms around the
biceps.
I wish they were showing in that picture.
Remember Bruce had a super fit body
in a book The Man Only I Knew.
In that picture if I had some way to expose the great feeling
about my tall part.
And the thing I want to change in my health is not to cough.
Look with those men of the body building magazine.
William L. Hogan, Jr.

Taking the next step is difficult when you don't know which direction to go. I would like to move from temporary housing to permanent housing. A place that's stable and close to stores. Since I don't
qualify for many of the housing programs, for various reasons. Where
do I go from here? How do I work toward this transition? I am unable
to work because I keep having strokes. Social Security keeps denying
me. I have a lawyer who says it may take a year to get approved. What
am I supposed to do for income? How am I supposed to take care of
my personal needs? It's rather embarrassing to have to ask others for
a roll of tissue or a bar of soap. How do I take the next step and the
road is so rocky. I know that God is carrying me through all this because I am so exhausted from taking the steps to get here.
Veyshon Hall

I feel like I am living in two worlds. One world is when I am being
in my classes. It's so peaceful and the environment is controlled.
Everyone is cooperative. Then I have to leave my class and go back
into the real world, where the atmosphere is not controlled. You never
know what is going to happen. It is unpredictable, unlike the controlled environment in the classroom.
Latasha Jackson

I'm sure no one woke up one morning and said, "Being homeless
is my new goal." If they did, I'm sure they're off their meds or in

need of a psych evaluation. The mental devastation is depression, anger/rage, disassociation, and suicide/homicide. The physical aspect, whew, is endless. The programs do what they can, with what they have. Everyone is not healthy, so germs spread. The stress level of not knowing contributes to heart problems and other health problems. In spite of the negative aspects of homelessness, there are many benefits that only the homeless receive. These benefits help us turn our muddy waters into Olympic gold opportunities.

Veyshon Hall

I do like to receive because
It makes me feel good.
I like to receive a new pair of lady tennis shoes.
That will make me feel good.
I would like to receive a new coat for winter.
That would make me feel good.
I would like to receive a new pair of jeans.
That would make me feel good.
I would like to receive a new tee-shirt.
That would make me feel good.

I would like to receive a new pair of gloves.
That would make me feel good.
I would like to receive a new make-up kit.
That would make me feel good.
I would like to receive a new hair style.
That would make me feel good.
My list of receiving can go on and on and on and on.
Oh,
I would like to receive a new dress. Thanks, that's all.
Oh, yes and some money – that would make me feel real good.
Jacqueline Crowder

I have great expectations for my life, even now. I never expected to be homeless, but just because I'm temporarily homeless right now, doesn't mean I'm helpless, or hopeless. I expect to have my own house soon. I expect to go to school so that I can better my life and fulfill my expectation to succeed. I expect my life to be great, exciting and fulfilling. I expect to get a lot of money so that I can help other people. I expect to travel to new places like Africa. I want to see those great big elephants. I expect to go to the pyramids. I expect to keep working to help end homelessness.
Latasha Jackson

During the periods of homelessness I didn't really care about much of anything but drugs and alcohol. My art work, philosophical thinking, and writing ability just got flushed down the toilet.

I did manage to keep clean and decently dressed by using the bathrooms at quick stop stores. They also furnished me soap or handwash which I used to take a stand up bath. I had fresh clothes stashed in various "cat holes". I always believed that if I didn't look homeless I wouldn't be treated as a homeless person.

This showed that I still had a bit of self respect left.

But looking clean and fresh is not only what self respect is about. I didn't respect my own virtues, talents, and compassionate nature. I had become too lazy and mindless to assert myself.

I did temp service work and used my meager earnings to buy crack, beer and vodka. I had no direction in my life and assumed that my life would end as a tramp. So I made no effort to get out of the rut I placed myself into.

Finally I entered a mental facility and discovered that I suffered from bi-polarism. A sense of worthlessness and fatigue. After being put on psych meds, my behavior did a 180 degree turn around. Now I can function on a rational basis.

I thank god for psych meds. Homelessness taught me that I needed help. I regret it took me so long to find out that I needed help.

Tommy Payne

This time last year I had my own house. Now my situation has changed. I'm thankful that I have a roof over my head. But I wish I still had my own house. I'm glad I have someone to help me. But I miss my independence.

I'm thankful that I will have a Thanksgiving meal. I just wish I had my own kitchen to cook my own meal. I have a locker for my clothes and I'm thankful for it, but I like having my own closet. I'm thankful to be able to take showers, still I miss having my own private bathroom. I'm thankful to have a bed. I'm grateful for being able to get clothes, I just want to be able to buy my own. I'm grateful to still have life but I want to have a better life than I have now.

Latasha Jackson

Walking is good for health and keeps you from getting sick but the sun has an effect if you stay out in it too long. But that cannot be helped and sometimes you can find shelter of some kind to keep out of the sun.

Anthony Johnston

When I became homeless in Tupelo, my most precious person in my life is my baby Tiana. It's now hard to leave her at my mother's home. I wasn't stable because I just had surgery on my right knee and I had just started to live in this house in Verona, Mississippi and it wasn't conditioned for a child to live in. When I move here in Memphis, my mother deceased so my brother has my baby Tiana. She turn 10 years old in June and I miss being a mother and knowing that nobody not going to take care of your child like you. But God has given me a reassure that in due season she will be back with me. Until then I am here to get the things I need to do and work very hard and determine to reach my goals. On this note I have to remind myself everything happens for a season, just a season.

Robbin K

Homelessness, I had a peaceful time going to the mission. The thing I didn't like - the trying to get a place to sleep.

William L. Hogan, Jr

Temples of the Mind
In the temple,
There is shelter;
From the sandstorms.
Here restless harpies,
And weary starlings;
Serve the darkness.
The sun
Never shines;
In the cold depths,
Of a broken heart.
The winds,
Speak unkind;
While shadows kiss—
And part.
And I only condemn myself.

In the gardens,
There are flowers;
Dressed like minstrels;
Blood red roses, deep blue violets,

Pure white lilies.
They sing—and they dance,
In my barren soul they thrive;
Then they bow, to the winds,
Praising god with their lives.
The only redemption,
That I have—for myself.

In the distance,
Purple clouds;
Chase the sunset.
Relentless hunter!
Soldiers of fortune,
Seeking power and glory
They'll run,
At the moon;
When the day hath waned—
And died.
But the chase,
Will be lost;
In the narrow room,
They'll hide.
Yet stroking—
And fondling,
Themselves.

In the valleys,
There are evils;
Dying children,
Ruthless leopards;
With bloody beards,
Gathering money.

My eyes,
Never cry;

They have seen the rages—
Of time;
We live,—and we die'
Without reason, fate, or rhyme.
There are others, so much—like myself.

Tommy Payne

What I lost when I became homeless was my doll collection. I really miss my doll collection. I had a few dolls that I collected that were special to me. I had a pretty black doll with kinky hair, which was my favorite. I had a musical baby that played Christmas songs and turned her head to the music. I miss my colorful doll that I sat on my bed. I also miss my other doll that I used to look at each day. Maybe one day I will have another doll collection.

Latasha Jackson

LATASHA JACKSON

I am Latasha Jackson. The most important event of my childhood was graduating from high school. I came to Memphis in 2009. My family lives in Louisiana, Texas, and California.

I was first without a place to live in 2009. I lost my job and my house. I was homeless for one year plus. My children were grown by then. I got my own house in August of 2010. I heard about the Door of Hope from a shelter worker. I started coming to writing group in 2009 when I was sleeping at the shelter. I kept coming to writing group because I enjoy writing and it gave me a way to express myself.

The hardest thing about writing group is transportation to group. My favorite topic is current events. If you think homeless folks being in a writing group is strange, I'd say it beats hanging out or stealing. My advice to others starting a writing group is to express yourself honestly.

The most important event in my adult life is seeing my children grow up and move on. Life is good—enjoy it.

DEDICATION
I would like to dedicate this book to my mom and my children

Elisha, Kieandre, Chandraneika, Nelwyn and Mack who inspired me to go on to achieve my best, and to keep reaching up, and to never give up.

CHAPTER 6
OUR DOOR OUT OF HOMELESSNESS

My difficult situation was when I had lost my house. I didn't know what to do or where to turn, or who to turn to. I had a panic attack. My friend helped me come up with a plan. He helped me to get my things put in place. He gave me money to stay in a hotel for a week. He helped me to buy food. He told me not to give up. He helped me to come back up. I really appreciate him being there for me. I don't know if I would have made it without his help.

Latasha Jackson

There was a time where I had no hope of getting out of being homeless. Then came a day when I had a moment of clarity, to ask for help! It really makes a difference when a person makes up in their heart to change something about themselves or situation like being homeless. With a little help from the agencies, to show you the right direction, to use these resources. I had to educate myself on how to get out of the problem, easier said than done, but with the resources I learned the steps to building up my self-esteem, self worth, morals & values, also the get-up-&-go to place myself back into society. Today it has gotten better & better because I am more responsible & caring about myself, also using my resources wisely.

Roderick Baldwin

Break of day are world of drugs
to keep our motor going and run

little animals away.
To keep hair animals lest in drugs.
Hester is longer run of all.
When water come longer run awfulest drugs.
Keeper, keep us healthy universal hold.
Hebrew prays God & Christ.
My Impact

                    Master Major Joshua Williams

I went into the Union Mission drug program in the year 2000. I was a cook there and the pastor was an ex-businessman now living in the mission. Not that he was homeless. He had a very nice home in Collierville. He just wanted to see how it was to be homeless and use it to start his own ministry. We became sort of friends, and he was very surprised at how smart I was. He said he was now feeling that god was calling him to preach and repent. And we are still friends. After 11 years.

I admire the pastor for being willing to go the length to do God's calling. He is the most down to earth minister I have ever met. He just talks simple, everyday talk and doesn't get way off in the universe to preach to homeless men.

I revisited the Mission this month and the pastor was still there caring for the homeless.

He was a lot of inspiration for me when I was battling addiction. I may need his inspiration again. I'm sure the pastor will be there for me.

                    Tommy Payne

My experiences as solo, being homeless on the street made my attitude very ugly as I was a monster! I came to realize it was my choice to do drugs and other things. As my girls started to get older, I had to make a decision to be a mother and lay all my trouble and cares to Jesus. I didn't want my daughters to see me as a monster on the street. As time went on my daughters still love me unconditionally even though I wasn't there for them all the time. The Lord has given me a new beginning in my life and he healed my relationship with my daughters. I am just grateful to be here today so I can help other people and give them the hope that they can make it with the Lord Jesus Christ being the number one creator of your life.

Cynthia Crawford

Being homeless, it was a bad time, but a good experience. We learn more and more and if not everyday it's sometimes maybe once a week. It's like you said, after we get placed we look back thinking it's not so bad. And I already know if we make a mistake we think, how did this happen? I was doing so good, at least I thought I was. But we also say to ourselves, things happen and knowing things just don't happen, our minds wonder like this. We try to figure it out and can't. No way!

p.s. I just thought of something the time after I said no way. I have a SOLUTION. We can draw and write and read how people escape to freedom. That will be the only way.

Anthony Johnston

At one point in my life I was homeless and really needed a place to stay. So one day a pal of mine told me about Manna House, a place where you could shower, change clothes, and get a hot cup of coffee and some positive conversation. At the end of a set time which is 11:00 or 11:30 they would close for the day, clean up, and get ready for the next day.

After they would be closed for a hour or two, the Door of Hope would come in and we would eat, talk, read and play some board games for about two or three hours. My first time there I met the director and her name was June Averyt. We talked a while and she wouldn't believe that I was homeless, and invited me to keep coming. Before I became homeless I was a cook at a local restaurant, and I saw that she needed a little help in the preparation of the meal. So I volunteered to make things better and everyone liked it, and a friendship was born. So in ending, June was there when I really needed a friend.

Leroy Scott

To end homelessness you have to have a job. Work in a specific field. I got out of homelessness by having a source of income. My income covers my rent. I feel my spending is not much. Going home can end homelessness and working. Parents do care about what happens to you in towns and cities.

Master Major Joshua Williams

If homeless people think of the welfare place and the welfare of their self they would get up and go to a place of help. Stop going to the eating place for a while and get to some place where they would take you in and talk to you about your homelessness. Find out of a home to go to. When I was homeless, I was going to some eating places and work a little and the churches. I got to know Miss June Averyt and am now in a home. So look for opportunity and you check into the things that would get you a home and check into you a home.

William L. Hogan, Jr.

After a few months of the Manna House we moved to the Church off Claybrook where the air conditioning picked up 100%. We had bigger couches and mattresses and a lot more privacy and TV, a great addition, and cooler people. After a month or so of that location we moved to the location on Bellevue where I became the Property Manager and got a room of my own. The air conditioning is great and so is the food and TV and a great society.

Leroy Scott

My life is gradually being transformed daily. I was needing to change some of my feelings about a lot of things. Now I'm beginning to see things differently. My attitude about some things is being transformed. I am being transformed to having a more positive attitude. I want to transform my life to be a positive influence for other people. My transformation has been coming forth for a long while. I believe I get a little more transformed every day. One day I will be totally transformed, like a butterfly.

Latasha Jackson

I am 31 years old. I am a Christian.
I am a white female. I am single.
I am not perfect.
I am beautiful inside and out.
I am homeless, but I won't be for long.
I have anger problems.
I often become depressed.
I am very smart and learn quickly.
I am a mother of 4.
I love to read.
I love to cook.
I have a one track mind and am easily distracted.
I hate conflict.
I also find it hard to find a good and true friend.
I love to drive as well as travel.
I have a heart that loves to help others.
I am working to become self sufficient.
I want to pay my own bills.
I want to provide for my children.
I want to leave government assistance behind.
I want my own income so that I may tithe.
I want to be able to go on family vacations.
I want to be able to give back to people and organizations that have helped me over the years.

So many different things that I am, I have, I want, I need, I love and I hate. Like a huge jigsaw puzzle, you have to take me a piece at a time. Some pieces are easier to work with than others. But I am getting there. Maybe faster or slower than you, which it does not matter. It doesn't make me better or less than you nor are you less or better than I am. We're just different. Isn't that wonderful! Imagine how boring life and this world would be if we were all the same. I think I would probably have difficulty dealing with that anyway. Seeing no one but a duplicate of me every day. Don't get me wrong. I am learning to love me. But that does not give you the right to hate me either.

I am who I am. Accept me as I am or watch me walk away!
Cynthia Crawford

I been waiting on Disability now for going on 3 years and in those 3 years I experienced quite a bit of things like thinking very negative thoughts and I'm not generally a negative person. I find that when I think negative thoughts, negative things generally happen and that's not good for me or anyone else.

So I saw that wasn't getting anywhere thinking like that. So I started thinking positive things about my situation and it seems overnight things started looking up. I started feeling better and everything started to fall in place, and a lot of positive things started to happen.
Leroy Scott

Now, in a homeless situation, I have found a career that I love. Helping others. Believe me, the work is hard, but the pay is super great. I receive many blessings, which is better than money.
Veyshon Hall

I like the quiet room. The time that I like at being sometime at the Door of Hope. I like the time of starting the day at the Door of Hope. I like the people and want them to take charge and get their things of the day and get to go with this and go the whole day at Door of Hope. The part for me is to come to writing class and do all of my subjects in the writing class.
William L. Hogan, Jr.

These are ways to keep a job. Have earned the trust for your bosses. Learn job information. Be on time for meetings and ask questions. Make and meet all payment plans. To keep your work schedule, do not be late. Make a friend. Just be outgoing and have fun at work to enjoy what you doing. Do not make errors.
Master Major Joshua Williams

Part I

I am going to be happy real soon. I am about to leave the place that I have been living in for 8 months. I am about to move into my own place. I can't wait to have some privacy. It's going to feel like heaven. I think I am going to fill the bathtub, light some candles, sit in the tub, and sip on some peach wine. It's going to be so nice to be alone.

Latasha Jackson, 2009

Part II

I'm keeping on keeping on working on getting my apartment. I can't wait to have my own apartment. I'm excited. It's getting close. I can feel it. I am going to keep on keeping on, waiting and praying for a nice apartment and I'm going to get one real soon.

Latasha Jackson, 2009

Part III

The thing that's most important to me right now is getting settled into my apartment. They have made me a happy woman today. I will be moving in a few days. I can't wait to fill my tub and get my peach wine and sit in the tub and sip it down slowly. Taking a shower is nice, but my feet are crying to be soaked in some water. I can almost feel the warm water on my body right now. A bath is going to feel so good.

Latasha Jackson, 2010

Every minor mistake I make,
They turn it around and throw it in my face.
    I must be doing something right.
For every successful moment that I have,
They immediately bring up my failures of the past.
    I must be doing something right.
I am closer to my higher power, more than ever
They shout, "It won't last forever."
    I must be doing something right.
I work the program, step by step,
They are eager for me to fall or slip.
    I must be doing something right.
I have a sponsor and multiple days clean,
They are still their old selves, not willing to change.
    I must be doing something right.
Yeah, I'm growing, changing and that's alright,
Therefore, I must be doing something right.

Veyshon Hall

It took a long time for me to realize that life is too short not to take it serious. Now I am facing my responsibilities as a woman and parent. It is never too late for your goals and dreams to come true. Since I have been here in Memphis, Jesus has opened up doors for me that I could have never imagined. In my mind I know he could not have done things for me, but I had faith and believed in walking in obedience. Now I can see my way and my eyes had been open into the world and I am not afraid and I have the courage to go through with my life. I can see myself prospering and enjoying happiness. I am being humble so he can use my ability to love people and help them.

    p.s. Thank you Lord for your precious blood.

Robbin K

When I was in the Life I wondered if I was in or out. People have so many outlooks on it.

But my feelings on this subject is, any day above ground is a good day. I enjoy myself and my friends daily when I can. So the question is who you want to be with, the haves or the have nots, and in a strange kind of way I manage to always be with the haves and that's a beautiful thing.

Leroy Scott

Now slowly day by day, step by step,
brick by brick rebuilding all that
was lost. She is gaining so
much more, than what was lost.
God's salvation to her imparts,
forgiveness at the ultimate cost.
Peace, Freedom, and love
beyond all human comprehension.
Jesus Christ's Life, death,
and ascension.

Cynthia Crawford

The thing about the Door of Hope is that they don't get on the homeless people caught in the tail of getting the service we provide. Not of the "we don't welcome the space of them." Get ready, we will wait for them to walk in. Like you will not feel stupid, just new people. Look all around, get the touch, and feel good. Walk through our doors feeling as tall as you make it. Thank you.

William L. Hogan, Jr.

WILLIAM L. HOGAN, JR

I am William L. Hogan, Jr. I was born in Memphis in 1959. My family lives in Memphis. The most important event of my young life was doing carpentry work like my father. The most important event of my adult life was growing to the age of 50.

I first became homeless at 16 years of age due to illness. I was homeless 9 years. I became homeless again for 12 years. I wasn't married and I have no children. I got into housing in 2009. I heard about the Door of Hope from June Averyt. I began coming to writing group in 2007. I was then sleeping at the Door of Hope. I kept coming to writing group because I was interested in it. What I enjoy most is doing the work—writing. There's nothing hard about writing group. My favorite topic is making a book. To those who think homeless folks being in a writing group is strange, I'd say, "Buy some of their material." If you are thinking about starting a writing group, I'd advise you to dig hard on the subject.

DEDICATION

The Door of Hope is for developing the hope of people who are homeless to be able to get a chance to get off the street. The trip we are taking on gives the welcome for a little vacation. This is a foundation made to give a person his chance to live.

CHAPTER 7
ALL IN A PIECE

JOCKLUSS THOMAS PAYNE: The Brass Menagerie

My wife, Marilyn Kathryn, was a collector of unique items. She had a knack for finding antique pieces that made great impressions on our friends. One of her proudest possessions was the Brass Menagerie. There was an elephant, a giraffe, a hippo, a rhino, an egret, and a few monkeys to grace our coffee table. Also two swans on our end tables. All of these animals were made of pure brass. Greatly detailed and in whimsical poses. We bought our brass zoo piece by piece. As well as gold-trimmed dishes to fill our walnut china cabinet.

"Miss Kat," as she was called, was a very fine homemaker with a graceful personality. For a Southern, Afro-American, she had exquisite taste and an uncanny ability to decorate. We had two Picasso prints plus my own artwork to give beauty and depth to our creativity.

Virginia Beach is a picturesque, small city, home to the sixth fleet of the U.S.Navy. Oceana, it is called. Norfolk completes the military district of Chesapeake Bay. I did many paintings of destroyers and aircraft carriers. Our house was like walking into an art museum and a naval academy at once. A unique combination. Juxtaposed between extremes; serenity and war. But what stood out most of all was the brass menagerie. They captured your attention above all the artwork in our home.

We moved back to Memphis in 1982. Her new location was Memphis Naval Air Station where she had moved up to EEO Officer. Tragically, my recreational use of cocaine and pain killers turned into pure addiction to the point of sticking the needle in my arms while my whole life went down the drain.

Use of cocaine, whether powdered or "rocked" is an evil, insidious practice. In my opinion cocaine is worse than heroin or morphine. It starts out as a fun, sexual stimulant. But as the disease progresses, it becomes an unnatural craving so intense that the user could possible kill for it. Slowly, our possessions began to disappear as I sat in the basement "shooting" cocaine for days at a time.

The brass menagerie. Where is it?!! Every person who has suffered drug and alcohol abuse has also suffered loss in one form or another. Loss of family, morals, friends, jobs, homes, status, and principles. I was no exception. I stupidly thought that the party could go on forever. AA philosophy states that you must hit rock bottom in order to recognize your own self destruction.

I never really hit rock bottom all through my struggle with drugs. Maybe in the sense of losing material things, but I never lost my basic convictions built around the victory of good over evil. I still practiced good in spite of my addictions. In this I found redemption, salvation, and the ability to overcome evil. I am still no saint. Not even a good Christian. I try to be on a daily basis. There are good Jews and Muslims. Buddhists and Hindus. I never based my recovery on religion or a "god" of my own understanding. I based it on the brass menagerie. Giving up things I truly adored to appease my unnatural cravings. My demonic cravings. I recognize the existence of evil. As long as I felt like there was no such thing as evil; a Nietzschean nihilism, I would have died as a crack addict or something even worse. I was headed in a dark direction. So I prayed to a god that is infinitely beyond my understanding or ability of conception. I cannot shape and mold god into what fits my understanding. If I could do so then the brass zoo could have been my god. Or the devil for that matter. After all, he too works in mysterious ways. He is a master of seduction and he rewards us with carnal pleasures. The same as god rewards us with blessings, material and spiritual.

I believe that I was predestined to follow a path towards truth and understanding. But I won't know god until I am totally with god.

I am still jostling around trying to make sense of my existence. Trying to find that certain person who will fulfill my life. Or that certain logic that will easy my prying, inquisitive mind.

This tightrope of life requires some sense of stability and purpose. Or else we give into the flesh and become homeless victims of utter worthlessness. We will give away all of our prized possessions but for a few minutes of pleasure. An escape from a reality that contradicts itself continually.

It may not be a brass menagerie, but we will sell our souls for a small price.

I remember like it was yesterday. I was sitting on the front porch of a dilapidated shotgun house surrounded by tall weeds. The house stood atop a deep ravine that had railroad tracks at the bottom. On each side of the trench were the same tall weeds littered by some colorless short trees. There were no lights on the dead end excuse for a street. The shotgun house was the only one occupied. The rest were vacant, crumbling sentinels to a gloomy, hopeless poverty.

Slinking cats prowled the weeds, their eyes glowing like sinister lanterns in the suffocating darkness of a tepid summer night. I fought ravaging mosquitoes that whined in my ears as I waited for the "dope lady" to bring me my "package." A twenty dollar "rock." I couldn't come inside for reasons that only the dope seller knew. I sat there impatiently as she took her time cooking up cocaine mixed with baking soda that made the soft powder crystallized into crack.

Headlights suddenly appeared then went out as the car parked in front of the porch. A young lady got out on the passenger side. She was about 22 years old with a figure like Venus and smooth black skin that glowed with vitality. She gave me that sex for drugs stare as she knocked on the door. She was a steady customer because she was let inside immediately while I had to wait outside on the porch infested with mosquitoes. I was getting more and more impatient. Finally the dope lady came outside and showed me her wares. "Venus" followed behind her, still having that "want do so something" look on her face. I declined the invitation. I knew that game well. I was no stranger to the ghetto. An empty promise. You get broke and still don't get what was promised. Only teased into buying more crack if you are that naïve.

From Virginia Beach to the shotgun house beside the railroad tracks. Rock bottom? Not quite. At least not for me. Not because my will was that strong, but god placed a shield in front of me where I could recognize how evil worked and brace myself against Satan. I knew what I was getting into. I would not get totally tricked and trapped into giving my soul over to darkness. Not even for a beautiful young woman. I was getting older. No more "Fat Tommy."

The brass menagerie still lingered on my mind. I hated myself for addiction. Coming away from that gloom and poverty was like waking up into the sunlight after a bad dream. I was destined to meet June Averyt and Ellen Prewitt. I was destined to do something meaningful with my life. My destiny had already been established. It was not my fate to end up in prison for the rest of my life or die in a meaningless incident resulting from addiction and crime. I have a message to deliver and god sustains me until it is done.

The brass menagerie is my reference point.

Since I've been rescued from homelessness I've had time to write about my experiences and do art work. I've joined church and become a Sunday School stand out. The world seems like a different place. A place where I can benefit myself and others. Instead of a bleak struggle to survive on a daily basis. From soup kitchen to soup kitchen. Chilling nights or mosquito infested empty buildings.

I'm a new person. One that has human dignity. Instead of hostile weakness from being crushed by society.

(portions of this essay first appeared in *The Bridge: The Memphis Street Paper*)

WJS

I remember my night of terror, the night I almost died. August of 1988, my husband attacked me. He beat me with his fists, punching me in my stomach and chest. He picked me up, arching my back, threw me down on the hardwood floor of our home in Denver, Colorado. I heard my back pop. It was a loud pop. Instantly there was this awful burning pain shooting through my upper torso. I could not feel my hip or legs.

I remember crawling, using only my arms and hands. I blacked out, and upon waking I crawled some more. I don't know how long that continued. I finally made it to the couch, tried to pull myself up and blacked out again. When I woke up, I was on the couch and he was undressing me. He carried my body to the bathroom and placed me in the tub, I think. The water was hot, but I could not feel my legs. I was terrified and completely at his mercy.

I blacked out again. He came and got me and took me to the bedroom where he put a gown on me and positioned me in bed. Then he brought the telephone and left the room. I picked up the receiver and was going to call the police and ambulance. But before I could dial 9, he came back in and snatched the receiver and slung the phone across the room and put a gun to my head. He told me he'll kill me if I turned him in.

I was terrified - mostly because of my children. I worried about them.

So it happened on a Friday. This day was Saturday when he pulled that gun on me and I couldn't do anything. Didn't have anyone to check on me. I was all alone. I prayed to God. I was unable to walk. He would bring my food to me that day. But I couldn't eat. So I was in and out of it all day Saturday. Sunday morning I awoke to breakfast in bed, and my first visit with my children. I hadn't seen them at all since that had happened. He told them I was sick. So I was in bed again all day Sunday.

I started positioning myself in bed to where my feet dangled off the side. Whenever he left the room he watched me, and would only let the children visit me for a little while. They had school on Monday. I made a plan in my head to try and escape. That Monday came. He let me call in to work to take the day off, but he forgot to move the phone. When he left to take the children to school, I started trying to stand on my legs to see if they would hold me. I did it in intervals because of the pain it caused me in my upper extremities.

By the time he made it back, I could walk slowly, taking 2 or 3 baby steps. I heard the door and I returned to the bed. I hadn't gotten completely on the bed. When he arrived in there, my legs were dangling. (The weight of legs that won't move is extremely heavy.)

He said, "What are you doing?" I told him I was trying to sit up, so he lifted me until I was in a sitting position.

That time in my life was the most painful and horrifying time of anything I had experienced. That is what someone did to me, his wife who he was supposed to love, and the mother of his children. I was also in shock. I didn't make it to a doctor until a week later.

There were peace in my house for some time after that. He started pampering me, paying more attention to me, telling me he's sorry. I accepted that, but I didn't trust him or know where he was coming from. I was always in fear of another of his outbreaks. Chastising myself for being in this situation with four small children, and nowhere to turn. So I thought at that time.I was in so much emotional pain. It was messing with my head. I believe that was when I became bi-polar manic depressed. For me I realized then that my life had ended.

I was getting up at 4:30 in the morning, heading to work by 5:00am, work eight to ten hours; go home and get ready for school (I went to college at night), and home at 10:00pm. Study for 1 hour and mingle with the children, getting them down for school the next day. By 12:00am I was in bed. Living on 4 hours of sleep each night, I was headed for destruction. So he brought it to me. Not because he wanted me to be with him, but for the fact that I had money. Money to supply his habit.

That's right, he introduced me to crack cocaine. One hit and I was hooked. It made me forget the pain I was in, the dead relationship and helped me to escape life. It also caused me a downhill spiral. I never hooked for drugs or stole, but I always worked, went to school and paid my bills.

Then, one day he got under my skin with his bickering, arguing about what he was going to do. I told him are you going to pay the bills, rent, light, phone, groceries? He said yes. I told him okay we'll see. So we got high and partied. We lost our home. And I told him I thought you said you were going to pay the bills. He looked like a wet puppy. Because he knew he couldn't pay. He didn't make that kind of money. I got tired of paying by myself. With him there so he would have to step up now and help some of the responsibility of raising a family.

As I recall more of my life, I remember Juneteenth of 1990. It's the celebration of the freeing of the slaves. He was getting dolled up. We had discussed about us going as a family, but he had other plans. So he left.

Well, I got the kids ready and we went. We saw him, and as he saw us. He became upset. (I guess because he couldn't do what he had wanted to do.) He started fussing and didn't stop until we arrived back home. (We were living in a 3 bedroom apartment then.) He jumped me as soon as we got home. I was scared. He made the children go to their bedroom, and he started hitting me. He turned towards the kitchen for something so I bolted out the front door running. I ran to the Safeway store that was across the street from my apartments. I used the pay phone to call 911.

As I was speaking to the dispatcher, I was looking around me and I saw him coming. I just dropped the receiver and ran. I ran up an alleyways, as he chased me, I ran in zigzag patterns, crossing block after block. I saw Burger King. I went in and told the lady at the counter to call the police. I saw him walking in the front of the store and got on the floor in the dining area. The manager came and got me and let me wait in his office until the police arrived. When they came, I told them how he was hitting and smacking me. And I told them my children was by themselves during all this.

They took me home. He had made it back. His eyes was blood red. They spoke to him, and noticed that the children had been left alone. They told him about it. Well, they allowed me to get some things for the children. And took us to the station first. Then they put us up in a hotel downtown and gave me some vouchers so I could get food. That started on a Friday also.

Saturday morning I took the children to McDonald's for breakfast. When we got back to the room, the older children wanted to see their dad. So I let them go see him on the condition they wouldn't tell him where we were. They came back, I said well did you get to see him? They said, "Yea," they was looking a little funny. So I said, "What's wrong?" My son told me, "Dad's downstairs." I told them, I told you not to tell him. They answered, he made them and walked back with them. We went back. Our life resumed and he started pampering me again. I didn't trust him any more and the more he started being violent, I started hating him. Through all of that I kept my job and he was working with a temp agency.

In 1991, I was working and the company got 6 tickets for my family for us to celebrate at Elitch's Garden. That was in June that year. We arrived at 10:00am, ate and enjoyed live entertainment and mingled with fellow employers and employees. The children enjoyed themselves immensely with all the rides they could ride. I rode one ride with each child and I let the older ones ride all the rides they could. We met back at the pavilion for lunch and drinks. They resumed their riding and my mate seemed to enjoy himself, especially since he could drink all the beer he wanted to drink. That evening we had dinner there and the children rode some more rides. We left the park around 10:00pm to go home. That night was joyous for all, for we spent it as a family, for probably the first time in our life.

Usually it was just me who did things with the children. I would take them to dinner and a movie on Saturdays, or to the State Building to tour it. I would let the children pick what they wanted to do on weekends, since that was when I had the most time to spend with them. Also, when my oldest son had games we went to them – he played little league football. His team won their division championship (my son was 8 years old then) and they won the Superbowl which we attended as a family. Well, my husband was mellow for yet another season. And I was feeling trapped more and more. The children wouldn't understand what I thought at that time about me and their dad's relationship. So I tried to keep a happy spirit for them.

I recall Halloween of that year (1991). I had decorated the house on the inside, with cobwebs, ghosts and witches. When the children made it home from school they saw it and their eyes lit up. They did their homework as I prepared dinner, made popcorn and placed treats around the house. They were excited and kept asking when Halloween was going to start. We started at 6:00pm. They went back and forth knocking on doors calling trick or treat. We gathered in the living room where we started in for a campout of movies and snacks. I believe they would all tell you that that was the best Halloween they had. For they had the both of us to themselves.

Well, by the end of November 1991, he had beaten me again, cracking my ribs. I could hardly breathe. But by the grace of God (he's kept me alive) I was able to carry on for my children.

I got a restraining order against him. Me and the children were placed in a home for abused women in Jefferson County. It helped me and the children cope during those traumatic times. The children were happier and smiling more. And I was learning that I didn't have to take that abuse. They started new schools and I found a new job working at this church for this cook named Bob (name changed). God put Bob in my life for a reason and to this day I'm eternally grateful for having met him.

Life was going pretty good for us. I was receiving counseling and so were the children. I had an attorney at that time to help me with the legal aspect. And we were progressing. The kids was thriving and I was happy for the first time in a long time since that happened. We spent Christmas and New Years there happy. Our time was running out there at that shelter in February 1992.

They placed us in another shelter. The children didn't like that one. So they were sad again. I kept working and picking them up and returning to that shelter. One day I saw a friend of my mate. He knew where I worked. Well, he told my mate and he started watching the place. One Friday he came to my job. My mate was one block away. His friend came to my job talking about my mate wanting his things back. I had to tell Bob my boss about what was happening in my life. I was totally embarrassed. We called the police, because I wasn't feeling safe. Upon their arrival, I told them about my restraining order and that I don't have his things. They spoke with him and after they left I told Bob I'm sorry that happened. I really loved my job. But, I'm going to have to quit. He told me they will make sure I'm safe there. But I explained to him that I know I'll be safe there on their property. It's when I leave that I was worried about. I was running on fear.

So now I had no job, staying in a place that made me and the children sad. I didn't know what I was going to do. During these trying times, I was so proud of my children for being able to tell me what bothers them about our situation, and that even in such harshness, we could find joy and still love one another. They helped me by not complaining all the time. By entertaining each other and keeping good grades in school and by being obedient children. God truly did bless me.

I went to work at a day care center, trying to secure a permanent job. During that time I ran back into my mate. He told me, "I've changed. Won't you and the children come home?"

Well, we did, but only to live with a friend of his. We paid his friend, an elderly man, to stay there. The children was happy to have that shelter, but they still did not like where we were. They had no sense of home, their home as a family. I agreed with them because I had no sense of home either.

Then one day my luck changed. I got a job with a company that made medical parts. With that check I could afford to pay rent. Finally we had two separate rooms. The kids enjoyed this better because it was just us – our family.

Trouble found me again. While I was working my husband was dabbling with drugs again. We would fight, but not so physical this time and that's a blessing in itself. While I lost that job due to tardiness (mainly because I was getting high), I thank God for that. Working with medical products, I could not take it if someone died from something I had made while high.

I tried to kill myself by taking a bottle of pills. He called an ambulance and he and a neighbor kept me walking – one on each side with my arms draped over their shoulders. The ambulance arrived and off we went to the hospital. They pumped my stomach and monitored me all night. I was disappointed I was alive.

I had gotten tired of him only wanting to get high and party, so as I was working day labor and coming back to the same old routine, I was mentally no good for anyone. I had to get away – get away to think and calm myself. I talked with my oldest two, and told them, I was sorry. I was not leaving them, just trying to change our living habits.

I left, so he was there to watch the children, and I came by daily when I knew he would not be there to see the children and pay on the rent, because he wasn't. I gave the oldest children the stamps to feed them with, only that he sold them.

I didn't miss the drugs or him, really, but it was tearing me up to be away from the children. One day while I was at work, he showed up and I told him I would come home. (God was working with me and I didn't even know it). He told me after I arrived that he called his dad and that him and the children were leaving the next day and that I could come if I wanted to. Of course I am going with my children so we packed and left the next day for Arkansas. We stayed in West Memphis, Arkansas in my mother-in-law's house.

The children went to school and was doing fine. I got a job at an all service, mini truck stop store. He was working at a detail shop off and on. We stayed there for two years. I called my father and asked him to come get us. He had started down the same road I was trying to run away from. My dad picked us all up in June of 1994 and we left to live in Atlanta, Georgia.

We moved in with my father and step-mother. We both started working at a day labor service, while he was looking for full-time employment. I got me a job at Kentucky Fried Chicken. We found us a unit at the Airport Inn. It was a one bedroom apartment. The children was in school and I thought we were doing ok. Our landlord called the Department of Human Services citing too many in one bedroom.

Well, they lost the case. I told the court that they didn't cite the Hispanics for having two to three families in one bedroom. Why were they citing me – because I am black? They dismissed the case. My unit was clean and they had food and were well cared for. The judge agreed with me.

I had found me a better paying job at a catering service for the airlines and had been working there for about 4 months. We were getting ready for our first Thanksgiving in Georgia. My mother had sent my cousin up that Monday to pick the children up. We were going to spend it together in Wrightsville, Georgia. The job would not let me off of work until the Monday after Thanksgiving.

Well, I was getting ready for work Thanksgiving morning of 1995.

My father came over to our place and he told me he had some bad news for me. He told me my mother had died that morning. I was in shock, angry and hurt. Confusion almost overtook me. Now, instead of going to spend time with my mom, I had to go to prepare for her funeral. I told my employer what had happened and we left for Wrightsville, Georgia – me and my husband. My dad did not cry.

The children were happy to see me, but they were saddened by what had happened. I am just glad my mother was happy before she left this world, and my children got another chance to be with her also before she left.

After we buried my mother, I didn't have enough money to bring us and the children back to Atlanta, so I asked the family to let them stay for about a month to give me enough time to save up the money to bring them back. They approved it, so I enrolled them in school and no one was to check them out of school – only for doctors' appointments.

Well, when I made it back to Wrightsville, Georgia, my children weren't there. I went to the police and they went and picked up my cousin and there I found out that my other cousin had transferred them to a different city with her. The police chief asked me if I might have any idea why they were running with my children across city lines. I told him no. He told me to go to the police department in the other city and that he was going to call ahead and let them know we were coming. He didn't want us going to my cousin's house alone.

To this day I am appreciative to the law department of Georgia, for they knew I was not doing anything wrong. I found out my cousin had filed abandonment charges on me. I was never informed. They knew where I was and what I was doing.

Well, we went to the Department of Human Services and told them everything that had happened and they told me and the police that those charges were unsubstantiated and that they see no case of abandonment in my situation. So the police department gave us another escort back to my cousin's house. She was told to have all of the children there when we got back. Oh yes – my dad took us both places. She got the children packed up and we left for Atlanta, Georgia again.

Back to my apartment. This was in February 1996. We enrolled them in school again. Everything was going okay until April. My oldest daughter called her grandfather in Memphis to come pick them up.

Well, I talked to him and he said they had plenty of space for them and they would like to have them there. I said okay. I talked to my oldest children and asked them why they had did that. They told me they were tired of being cramped up and it's been hard on them. So I told them I don't have to let you all go but I love you all very much so I am going to let you go stay with your grandparents, at least for now, and we will join you all later.

When they left, I was lost completely. My motivation was gone. I didn't care if I had a roof over my head or not. Now I'm in Atlanta very depressed, confused, and not really knowing what I am going to do, so me and my husband stay in the apartment until we have to exit due to no payment. So we went to the day labor company and waited to get a job. We would wait until they called our name. If they haven't called your name out by 9A.M. there's usually no more tickets for that day, so we would wander around. When night came, he found this place where they parked school buses, so we slept in them for about two weeks. We never got there until after 10pm and we would leave at 5am to get to the labor pool place.

We did that until these savages found the place and trashed the bus. We found that out by walking past there one day and the police were doing an investigation. People again can be so cruel. So we had to find us again somewhere else to sleep and that helped us a lot, being that it was winter. We had us a spot we could shower at so we showered every other day. We communicated our happenings only to each other, but to others we looked like we still had a home. We carried only one small bag apiece.

So we found this lady who ran somewhat of a crack house. After we showered we would go to the store to get my husband a beer and head up to the house where we started the ritual of getting high. We'd sleep sitting up until time to leave – usually 4:30 am or 5am.

We would also put our money together to eat, get a hotel room when we could so we could maintain our body hygiene. I didn't care to be stinky and raggedy. I cared enough to know I had to try to stay healthy for my children.

I wrote letters to the children and I would call to let them know I still cared for them and for them to know I am alright. The more I spoke with them the more depressed I became. Finally, in November of 1999 I left Atlanta, Georgia, boarded a bus for Memphis, Tennessee to be with my children. Two months later my husband decided to join us. The kids were happier but I was miserable. I was happy to be with my children, but I was miserable because of my situation. Something had to be done.

ROBBIN K

I have told you part of my story about moving to Portland, OR at 20 years old to move in with my brother and becoming homeless. I would jump the train there with other homeless people and stay in different shelters, because I was running from myself and not to do the right thing. Eventually one day I was tiring of getting high so I made a phone call there at my brother's house. But I didn't know that my parents were there looking for me. God works in mysterious ways to get our attention. One of the verses in bible says, Be still and know that I am God. He wants to have a fellowship with us, so we can come to him for help and our needs. But I wasn't trying to hear that. So I moved back to Flint, Michigan, and stayed with my parents. But I continued to get high so my mother put me out of the house. So I hit the street for about 15 years. My drug habit became worse. I lost my apartment and my self-esteem, so I hit the street and became a prostitute.

Crack cocaine was my drug addiction. It made me do some things that I never imagined doing. But I would go to church and was still crying out to God because I knew the master was the only one to bring me out of my addiction.

I started to have kids. So I had two beautiful daughters and I couldn't take care of them as a mother because I was just crack out. So my parents got custody of my two daughters. But being out in the streets, I was into tough times, fighting, stealing, and I stopped caring about myself as a person; I just didn't care about life period. So I became a monster. When I first started to get high, I loved it, but over the years I started to hate it because I was hurting my daughters and family. But I started to pray and ask God for help, because I wanted to stop running from him and wanted to be a mother to my daughters.

I went to 4 treatment centers. It didn't work because I wasn't ready to stop. So one day I ask God to take the drug, alcohol, and my lifestyles out in streets. I used to sleep on benches on the river and abandoned houses too. It started with me & 20 women on the street. But Jesus heard my cry and I met this pastor at home and he told me about this placed called Hannah House Ministries in Detroit, MI. So I went there for 9 months. That's when I got in tune with myself and Jesus. He show me a whole lot about me. He loved us so much that we can't not love our self. My parents was proud of me. I learned responsibility in my life and I stopped running from it. Me and my daughter started a good relationship. I am not perfect because I was in and out my daughter's life, but god saved me and made a way in my life again.

Without the master love we cannot do anything without him. He show me to love myself again and there is hope, patience, and endurance.

I ask my parents for forgiveness for all the things that I put them through and when Jesus delivered me off drugs, that it was the best thing to ever happen to me. When you are homeless out there in the street, people look at you nasty and talk about you and even your family becomes your enemy. I learned how to survive out there because God showed me and gave me the wisdom. It's not a good feeling because you lose focus about yourself and depression, loneliness, and low self esteem and the main thing you lose is hope. You cannot lose hope out there, because the weak always go on the waste side, but the strong survive. I thank God for my experience in the street because I learned so much about myself and people. God always has a plan for your life, you are the one to ask God for your purpose in this world.

My mother became real sick in 2003 so she wanted me to move back down south in Tupelo, MS, to be close to her family. She was on kidney dialysis for 9 years. By that time I had another daughter. My daughters names are Wanakee, Asha, and Tiara. I stayed home with my parents, but some people can't let the past stay behind. When somebody has something over your head that reminds you of things in your past and continue to drill it over you. But God in his word, he is a forgiving God no matter what you have done. You read John 1:9. He is faithful to us till the end. So I left my parents' house and became homeless again in MS. I met a friend in Vernon, MS. This house was abandoned, but he told me the lights, gas and water was still on in the house. So I moved in there for 3-1/2 years, but I was still crying out to God. He (God) told me and my friend to jump to Memphis, TN.

We did and in the spirit I felt the chain was broken off of us. I arrived in Memphis, TN, and I went into a shelter called Sister's. It is run by nuns. And the Lord bless me to go farther in another sheltered called Salvation Army. I meet two ladies there who the Lord blessed in my life so I can go on to pursue the things I need. During that time I called back home and my oldest daughter told me my mother passed away. It was devastating to hear that. But one thing I learned over the years, drug and alcohol can't fill that void, but Jesus can. He kept me in perfect peace to go through my mother's death. So I was blessed with an apartment by an agency named Door of Hope. They help me with housing and utilities. So I step in faith and move to a different place and make a sacrifice for the Lord. He has opened up doors that men cannot open.

Once you know who you are in Christ, can't nobody take anything from you, and you have a voice in this world, don't let nobody tell you different.

You follow your heart and dreams, when you put your mind into it with your body, soul and spirit, you cannot lose with master, and that's Jesus Christ.

I thank God for allowing me to write my book. Because people need to be set free and Truth that they can make it through Jesus Christ.

1 COR 9

I love Jesus and trust in him. He made me to be a better mother and person. I have peace in my life and restore my relationship with my daughters.

Key to Jesus is praying. When we get down on our knees, praying changes things in our life. I am a better woman today, am clean, delivered and saved through Jesus' precious blood.

I thank Jesus keeping me safe and saved. The program I am in, Door of Hope, we have a writing group and I always told my daughters that Jesus was going to make a way for me to write a book about my life. I spoke that into existence years ago. Now it has come to pass. Jesus always give us a promise in his word. He promises me everything I lose will be given back to me in triple.

ROBBIN K

I am Robbin K. I was homeless for 15 years. I was born in St Louis, Missouri. I was the only girl in my family, and I was spoiled because of it. I moved to Memphis on September 9, 2011. My family lives in Tupelo, Mississippi and different places. I was nineteen years old, in 1986, the first time I was without a place to live. I became homeless when my parents kicked me out of the house. I was homeless for 3 or 4 months. I have three children: all girls.

I got into housing in February of 2012. I heard about the Door of Hope through the Salvation Army and began coming in December of 2011. When I first joined Writing Group, I was sleeping at the Salvation Army. I kept coming to writing group because I was interested in writing. Mostly, I enjoy hearing everyone's stories. The hardest thing about writing group is putting your feelings on paper. My favorite topic so far is a book about me. To those who think homeless folks in a writing group are strange, I'd say, "It's not strange, it's just putting your feelings on paper." To others thinking about starting a writi-group, I'd advise them to be yourself, be open with your writing. The most important event in my adult life is being clean and sober and having housing. I thank God for the Door of Hope and its ability to house the homeless.

DEDICATION

I would like to dedicate my book to my children and my mom, Reola K. She was the one to teach me how to stand strong in my opinions. Learn me how to become a woman and respect myself and people. Taught me to be a mother to my kids and taught me to be responsible in my life and stay focus on things and learn me to go out and get it, not to be a lazy person and always to take care your business in the morning. And when life attacks you in different areas of your life to always have Jesus number one first in your life. To guide you and to establish a prayer life. I was blessed to have my mother for 73 years on earth. I know she is always in my heart and spirit everyday. Thank God for Door of Hope writing group and agency to receive me and given me another chance. Thank God for Salvation Army and Sister's Shelter.

CHAPTER 8
CHANGES IN OUR LIVES

I like the change in my life to be able to wake up in a warm apartment, not a bench or a house with no water or light or gas. Now the Lord has blessed me with water, light and gas and being able to cook and take a nice warm bath and have clean clothes.

Since I stepped in faith last year in September to come to Memphis to live, life has been changed in me, like having a relationship with my family, and talking with my daughters and meeting people in Door of Hope to make that change for me. Life is a breath of fresh air and don't take it for granted. Just take one step at a time with Jesus.

Robbin K

Change is hard depending on where we are, if you ask me. I say this because I was at the motel and I made that change and it really was not hard at all. That's the reason I say depending on where we are to make a change.

Anthony Johnston

Everything is wet from the rain. There is steam rising from the slick, shiny street. Birds are singing everywhere. The sky is bluer than blue. There are pretty rainbows to chase. Some lives were lost and many were saved. We know that there is chaos and confusion during the storm. Then we must also admit, there is beauty after the storm.

Veyshon Hall

It's 8 am in the morning. He prepares himself for a day at the Support Center – the hygiene and the clothes he prepares for the Day! He gets in his car – man of color he looks forward to a day of people in need! He makes coffee, sets-up the Center to be cozy! Prepares a nice lunch for the guests to enjoy! Being an example for the ones down on their luck – he hopes to give them hope through communication and listening, showing that someone cares for them! Building health and personal relationships is health for the Soul! We all sit down and have lunch together like a family. We all come from different walks of life, but we have a lot in common. The Center gives all an opportunity to read, write, and feel important about self and others! It really helps, to get out of self and help someone else. Thank you Door of Hope! For helping all people!

Roderick Baldwin

I wake up. I praise God for this beautiful day! I shower and prepare for the day. I praise God for the energy to complete the day's tasks! I board the MATA bus to start the day's journey. I praise God that he is guiding me! I check my e-mail, update my résumé, and complete some job applications. Praise God for all he has done, is doing, and will do. I go to the local mission and get fed spiritually. Praise God for Jesus's gift to us all! Then I get fed beans and weenies, cole slaw, corn, and cheesy garlic bread. Praise God for providing not only what we need but sometimes also what we want! I leave and ease on over to Door of Hope. I praise God for people that care and truly help others in need! We here at the writing group write, read, and inspire. Praise God for my family here at Door of Hope and the writing group!

Cynthia Crawford

My SSI check has been a great help to me. It has helped me to buy soap, toilet tissue, PineSol, bleach, washing powder, toothpaste and also pay bills. I wish it will never stop coming. It is truly wonderful that this could happen to me.

Jacqueline Crowder

It is a blessing that I can rent a room to do my sports in. A blessing and you can do a workout. I do work outs in football, boxing, and basketball. I have a record keeping of time-after-time shooting in the goal here. I'm sturdy and have a ball. I have good moves in the sports. I have improved my karate. In a workout I have a coach work with me. I am a starter. I'm about six feet seven. At a Health Clinic I was told that I am 81 inches 6 feet 9 that comes to be because I do professional workout. I tighten up and do body building in my mirror. Everything is fit. It is good that I don't have an impossible picture. It is a blessing I keep my back straight and the house has a 7 feet door frame to keep busy with.

William L. Hogan, Jr

Before I couldn't get to a gym like most people because I had no income and could not afford the fees. So basically I had to stick to walks in the park. Occasionally some parks had exercise bars like the one near Ed Rice Community Center, so I got to work out my arms and legs. I would also play basketball and catch with a dodgeball to get more exercise. Now that I am housed, I got another set of weights. I had to give my other set away because they were too heavy to carry around all the time. I also do yoga once a week, which is very hard to do if you're homeless because the classes are usually for pay, but this one's free so I could have done it when I was homeless.

Tamara Hendrix

Growth, well! Growth is a great thing. Now myself in particular I've grown up, down and all around. The up side really amazes me because June pushes me so much subconsciously I learned patience, thoughtfulness, understanding and aggression. The down side: humility, inquiring thoughts, and decision making. All around side: real love and understanding for my brothers and sisters.

One thing that really amazes me is how I've gone from cooking for myself and my sisters to cooking for 2 to 3 hundred people every 5th Sunday. I am blessed to be in charge of cooking for 2 to 3 hundred people at Grace-St. Luke's. So far, by the grace of God, I've had nothing but rave reviews and it makes me want to do my very best to satisfy my guests.

And the most amazing and interesting is that how I came to grips with people who have mental disabilities and somewhat psychotic and bi-polar personalities. Being very patient to really listen and to comprehend to the best of my ability.

Leroy Scott

I spent time being homeless for a little over a year. I am so grateful for my apartment. It was awful living in a shelter, being told what to do. I'm so glad I can cook my own food. The food at the shelter was really awful. I used to hate having to have cereal every morning. It was really hot in the shelter. I'm so glad I can live in air condition comfort now. I'm glad I don't have to hear someone coming in really early telling me it's time to get up. (Now I get up early by choice). I'm glad I can cook when I get ready, instead of someone telling me it's dinner time. I love being able to take a bath instead of a shower. I can't wait to get my money, so that I can sit in my tub and sip my peach wine.

Latasha Jackson

This morning was the sweetest morning over at Door of Hope. Drinking water and taking my medicine was the first thing I did. After five minutes of painting outside, I was wet. I am having a better day because of the air inside.

Looking forward to a cool winter day. Cool sand winds that flow and blow to keep sand and grass in place. In places where I live the most.

Master Major Joshua Williams

I'm thankful for my hands—that I can use them.
I'm thankful for my arms—that I can use them.
I'm thankful for my fingers—that I can use them.
I'm thankful for my legs—that I can walk.

I'm thankful for my feet.

I'm thankful for hair on my head—that I can comb it and style it.

I'm thankful that all the activities are working on my body.

I am thankful for my eyes, ears, and nose, and the teeth in my mouth—that I can eat the good thanksgiving feast.

In Jesus's name we pray. Amen.

Jacqueline Crowder

My favorite room in the Door of Hope is the kitchen because I love to cook and to see people eat and enjoy. I also love to prepare coffee for a couple of my roommates, William and Mike. I also like washing my clothes and drying them and generally washing the dishes and keeping the kitchen clean.

Leroy Scott

The most important thing to me is to keep my mind on my living. If I keep my mind on the thing I do, I can keep up. All the things I do are by the mental operation. I must keep my thoughts going. If my thinking stops, I will not be able to function at all. I use my mental part of life, I will keep my physical part of life going, doing work and moving. Keep all my certain projects and programs going right.

William L. Hogan, Jr.

I can't truthfully say that Jesus Christ changed my attitude about myself. But what he represents, absolute love, gave me an incentive to become Christ-like in my feelings towards others.

I feel good about myself now. I am nowhere near perfect, but I strive to reach a higher ground on a daily basis. Keeping my thoughts on a positive level and doing whatever I can to help those in need.

I had considered myself a total failure up to my acceptance of the Christ emblem as a way of life.

For the past 17 years, I have not awakened in a jail cell or felt guilty over my character. I'm a long way from perfect, but perfection is a lifetime goal.

Perfect faith, perfect charity and perfect love.
I hope to come close.

Tommy Payne

In the last year I got off drugs, got housing and a fresh piece of mind. I was unhappy most of my life. Now I am happier than I have ever been in my life. Life has been very hard but thanks to my belief in God and knowing that he has my back, things are better for the first time in my life. I feel loved. The Door of Hope did that for me. I never believed that people who don't know me could love me. I looked for love from men and got nothing but pain. So I am glad that this change came unto my life. I love you, Door of Hope.

Donna Connie

Recovery is a process; I know, because I am recovering from things in my life

The process of recovery for me was accepting the condition or what's happened to me. For me, too, recovery is a healing process - a lot of reconstruction. Mentally, physical, emotionally. There have been a lot of things and people I have lost in my life or gave away! To recover I cannot do it alone; learning how to deal with what was lost and how or what's important for me to recover.

Starting over in life.

Recontacting relationships.

Getting a mindset on working for what I need.

Getting help in my recovery process.

Taking a look at what areas I need to improve.

Time heals wounds - God takes care of that!

There are so many areas people are working on to get better in. And learn how to cope with something bad has happened to the individual. For myself - I will be getting better hopefully one day at a time. The world does recover, people, homes and lives. It's part of our life of survival to go through things but to recover is a beautiful thing.

Roderick Baldwin

This is the way I feel about now. I sit here and think about my life. It was not a pretty one but I endured a whole lot. Sometimes it was up and down because all the trials and tribulation I went through. Today I can see myself with confidence and hope. To encourage other people there is hope. When you set your goals in your life and accomplish them. That's a real good feeling you can make it or be somebody.

Somebody told me in my past, you don't have no voice, but you do. When somebody come to you with negative thought or action, you have to be able to stand strong enough and tell yourself you do have a voice in this world and you do love yourself, no matter what happens in your life. When God gives you another chance to breathe his air and get you up with a sound mind and health, that's your chance to move on with a positive thinking and action, so you can endure the fight and race to conquer anything in life you can set your mind to.

Robbin K

The worst thing that can happen to me is someone trying to change me. The way you look, act, talk and feel. To be yourself is the best thing, that you as somebody can be. Just know, you don't look like a fool or smell like dirt.

The bigger change, moving in the house with the long list of rules. I can live with that because it beats being homeless. My image has changed. I'm light on my feet, I stay upstairs. It's nice (ok) the new house.

Master Major Joshua Williams

All my life I have been searching for a career. I have so many gifts, I was confused. I have worked up and down the work scale, job and money wise. None of them satisfied me, I was bored and would move to the next job. Now, after almost killing myself working, I have a part-time job that is satisfying and very flexible.

I am assistant manager at a home for disabled adults. Wow. Go figure. I'm helping myself and others. I'm not just a client, I am now a proud Door of Hope employee. Yep, I get to give back to the organization that gave me so much. Being homeless was a shock, but finding a job in that, priceless. They say that nothing from nothing leaves nothing. I beg to differ. Nothing from nothing leaves hope. Door of Hope. That is.

Am I satisfied? Well, yeah. And the blessings just keep flowing and flowing and flowing.

Veyshon Hall

The most dramatic thing that's happened since I've been housed is that I don't have to find places to sleep or resources. I am constantly reminded of the different paths I can take since this one door has been opened and one obstacle is conquered. I have adapted well back into a "home setting" and will continue to at least try to remain positive in the sense that this could lead to a new beginning for my life, instead of the negative things that come with being homeless.

I had a very emotional reunion with my son. Seeing him for the first time in 2 years made me very happy and joyful. My life is coming together now and we spend time with each other all the time and he tells me everything is fine. He knows this is "recovery" for me and that I am doing the best I can. Life on the streets has taught me to appreciate those who love you, no matter what situation you are in, and to treasure those that want to help you better yourself.

Tamara Hendrix

Being housed is a blessing. It makes you feel so good knowing that you have a roof over your head and food to eat, clothes on your body, shoes on your feet and soap to wash your body. No one to wake you up at 6:00 in the morning. I can do this and that in less than 24 hours.

Jacqueline Crowder

I remember the time when I had started with the Mission ten years ago. I am now having another year and in the eleventh year. I noticed change and growth of the six places where I have been going. The new change in good is in September. I will have a change in growth.

I will be 50.

William L. Hogan, I

One of my favorite places to be is at a friend of mine named Paul. His grandfather has a farm with a pond on it full of bream and catfish. He also has ducks, chickens, horses, pigs, cows, bulls, guineas, goats, and geese and a few more things. I love the smell of the fresh cut grass, the cool breeze on the pond and the smell of the fish.

He also has an uncle that owns a restaurant and on a long day he brings us lunch that is always tasty and nutritious. The farm is on 500 acres. Beautiful trees, sprawling grasses and shady.

Leroy Scott

My favorite place in Memphis is the old river bottom west of the Thomas Allen steam plant. The Chucalissa Indian Village is in the same area. I'm not particularly fond of the steam plant, but of the vistas of wild flowers and the broad expanse of McKellar Lake. Complete with brooding forrest. The old river bottom is a great fishing hole. I'm an avid fisherman and it is teeming with gamefish. Like bream, crappies, and yellow perch. Catfish also abound as well as carp and buffalo. On a good day I can eboat about seventy or eighty fish. According to the strange temperament of fish. Some days they will bite and some days they won't.

There is also the plaintive cries of jackdaws, and doves. Ever so often a crane will fly over. Bound for I don't know where but giving a graceful, muted echo to the sweet songs of nature.

I feel as one with nature and it is the most peaceful place on earth, next to cemeteries. There is a feeling of oneness and serenity. The plop of feeding fish breaking the silver green water, a mosquito shines in your ear. A cotton mouth slivers through the peaceful water in search of a hapless frog.

I love this kind of communication with life. I can't wait for Leroy, Premus and myself to visit the old river bottom. We country boys will perhaps bring in loads of fish. Like we did last year and the year before.

Tommy Payne

FONDEST MEMORY

I got a job working at a dollar store. We had more than 1 job. Mine was cashier, stock the front of the store and watch for shoplifters. I told my manager: I was not going to fight with shoplifters anymore! Well let me tell you something. One morning right after we opened, this man came in and I saw him shoplifting so I called for price check (code for shoplifters). My manager was coming to the front when this man started to the door. The manager said, "Lock the door," so I ran to the door and was locking it when this man slung me across the room. By then the manager got there and was fighting with him. So I ran to the phone and dialed 911. They got there in about 2 minutes. They arrested the man, and when it was all over—the manager said let's go have a cig. While we was sitting outside I told him, "I'm not going to ever do that again." He said I don't blame you and we smoked our cigs and then reopened.

Rhonda Lay

I was approved for disability
I'm glad about it.
I can move, maybe buy a car.
But wait, stalled from the start.
There is a snag, in the payments.
Broken down in installments?
This will not do.
So God, as always, I'm depending on you,

I say.

God replies, I already did that, next.

Veyshon Hall

I think recovery is a beautiful thing. It's like you have been given a second chance, a chance to build back stronger. I had an aneurism three to four years ago and I'm still recovering from it now as we speak. I know that I lost a lot of memory and other things. Sometimes I feel weak and sometimes I feel stronger but mostly I feel blessed because I learned that most people don't live through them so I feel truly blessed. I'm also recovering from two heart attacks and two strokes, which I don't think I will ever get over.

Leroy Scott

What I do to stay healthy is taking my blood pressure medicine every day. I have to take my vitamins. I have to eat right. I started to eat fruits and vegetables more. I don't eat junk food any more, except for occasionally. I take daily walks. I recently had my cholesterol and blood pressure checked, and they (the doctors) said that it was good. I have to have regular checkups to make sure I stay healthy. Sometimes when I get stressed, I have to find a quiet place to get away so that I can think, meditate and pray.

Latasha Jackson

What I would look at to say Memphis is good. I would look at if the city has busing. I would look at if the television has top playing picture on television, how much of a sports city it is, if the city has a YMCA or do the city got opening on the weight room. What kind of activity clubs are in reach. How much traffic the city has, is there a lot of jobs, any well-known coaches and a way to meet active people. This will be easy.

William L. Hogan, Jr.

What I do with my time, mostly a lot of things at the Door of Hope: cooking, cleaning, maintaining the peace, gardening, collecting

135

the mail, and being a basic overseer of the Door of Hope.

Now I also have a friend of 30 years or more that has moved back to Memphis from Chicago and we do a lot of cooking and grocery shopping. We also ride around and see old friends, hang out at his job and run various other errands. Some days I eat and look at TV a lot. Sometimes before my bike was stolen I would ride over to some of my other friends' houses and talk or whatever.

Leroy Scott

My days are spent doing from one thing to another. Working crossword puzzles, drawing pictures, tending Door of Hope Gardens. I'm not much of a T.V. fan but when there is nothing else to do I do watch late night shows, especially Perry Mason. Oh yes I do have a strong interest in law, rules of evidence and legal citations. I guess you might say I am very versatile and interested in almost everything. I read a lot and ponder many subjects from the universe to microbiology. In short I do a little bit of everything and whole lot of nothing.

Tommy Payne

Well, for me my something special happened yesterday. We were on an outing—when I say we I mean the Writers Group. As I was saying the outing was great. First we went to the Caritas House for a fabulous lunch where the burgers and bread pudding was delicious. Then to STAX Museum. It was my first time back to STAX since it was re-opened again from the early days of the '60s and '70s. We used to go to the back door and peep in on Isaac Hayes, David Porter, the Bar-Kays, Otis Redding, the Dramatics, Temprees, Madd Lads, Rufus Thomas, Sam and Dave, and many more great artists.

For some reason, my favorite artist was Isaac Hayes. He was such a dynamic individual. Bald head, long gold chains and a real deep voice with great lyrics. I was knocked off my feet when I saw Isaac Hayes' custom El Dorado trimmed in gold with the white mink carpet and the bar in the back and the TV in the front. I remember when he used to drive it down the street, it was such a beautiful sight to see.

Leroy Scott

Taking a trip to STAX Museum filled me with a lot of nostalgia. During the heyday of STAX, I was about fifteen years old and I lived very close to STAX Records, about two blocks down the street. I was able to hang around the studio, run errands for the singers and musicians, and actually sit in on recording sessions.

What is most memorable about STAX Records is how it developed the talents of many aspiring performers who otherwise might not have become famous. STAX produced a distinctive, soulful, delta, gritty form of rhythm and blues that became world famous and brought to Memphis a place on the world map as the home of soul. Plus the fact it was a bi-racial effort in a time of racial strife. STAX will always be remembered in that respect. It also must be remembered as a big business organization that propelled many of its performers to financial heights never before achieved in the blues delta circuits.

It would take a book to re-live all my experiences at STAX Records. But I will say that it gave a great deal of cultural, musical, and racial pride in that STAX was able to bring whites and blacks together and produce a world famous sound known as the "Memphis Sound," my adopted home town.

Tommy Payne

For a long time, I have always wanted to see and learn about the STAX history. Hearing about STAX through others made me very interested. I have heard a lot of the music, from Isaac Hayes, The Bar-Kays, Staple Singers, Memphis Horns, Sam and Dave. The music I was listening to was telling a story about life and its experience. The music touched my soul, it had sound all by itself. The emotion it brought out was a good feeling. The music told personal feelings and experience that I can experience. No color or stigmas was here; the joy that music can bring. How the STAX experience brought people together in music. Going to STAX myself brought back the times of clothes, hair styles, a different style of music. Brought back childhood memories of peace and good will. All that different culture coming together, to share their life and love of music, and the messages it gives us. The STAX experience is something we can build on to help people understand that through music we can change and bring people together. I'd heard of Isaac Hayes because his sister and brother went to Manassas High School with me—being across the street from Isaac Hayes' grandmother. Seeing the Cadillac he drove when I was in my teens. In my life I have had the opportunity to meet Rufus Thomas and his children and Isaac Hayes—James Alexander and Larry Dodson of the Bar-Kays, some of the Mitchells—the pioneers of the STAX experience. It was and still is an honor to have met and listen to their experience of the times we left behind—but through the STAX museum we can re-live the good times. And help touch and pass the hope and dreams of the pioneers of change and togetherness. Thank God for the STAX experience and the people who are still keeping it alive.

Roderick Baldwin

I walked through the Pink Palace and saw hundreds of objects. Everything was in neat order and I liked the people sitting in the set up houses and the moving dinosaurs. I liked the adventure set up there because it was new. I walked through the place thinking about the muscles of the body and picturing the muscles in my mind.

William L. Hogan

I enjoyed my visit to the Pink Palace Museum for the historical information I learned. Especially the history of the Civil War. I have read many books on the subject but seeing the soldier uniforms and the actual weapons used to fight with made me think of the bloodshed and carnage this war shed. I was amazed that 600,000 soldiers died in this war. Along with the famines and diseases that costs thousands of more lives.

The dinosaur bones and plaster figures made me realize that god thought of everything. He created bones that do not deteriorate like flesh so that we could reconstruct them and have an idea of what reptiles looked like millions of years ago.

The log cabins and furniture of the 19th century were very exquisitely made of the finest woods and fabrics. The styled chairs, desks, and cabinets were so richly adorned and artistically styled. As a once antique dealer I wished I could somehow get ahold of these furnishings and sell them for outrageous prices.

Then there were the collections of butterflies and different species of roaches. I love butterflies with their brilliant colors and patterns. I hate roaches. They drive me crazy. But they too have a place in the strata of life As well as flies and mosquitoes. What are their purpose? Only god knows.

Tommy Payne

I enjoyed visiting the Pink Palace museum yesterday. The national history of science and cultural. I saw old timey refrigerator, old typewriter, and old clothes and shoes that they wore back in the days. The most exciting part was those beautiful lighted Christmas trees and the music playing in the background. Maybe if we're good we'll get a chance to see it next year. Until then, Merry Christmas.

Jacqueline Crowder

Yesterday I went to the Pink Palace. I really enjoyed it. I liked looking at the fossils and bones. I wondered what life must have been like back then when dinosaurs roamed freely. I saw a buffalo, a grizzly bear, and a black bear. I pictured myself on a safari in Africa. Then I went upstairs and I saw the beautiful Christmas trees. I felt like I had made a visit to Christmas land. They had a Care Bear tree, an Autism tree, a tin soldier tree, and other beautiful trees. My favorite was the baby doll tree. It reminded me of my best doll collection.

Latasha Jackson

Visiting Mud Island was such an adventure. Being high in the sky riding the monorail was exciting. Maybe one day it will be a rocking monorail, just kidding. There was plenty of fresh air and plenty of beautiful pictures to take. The boat at the Riverboat Museum seemed real. When you closed your eyes and listened, you could almost feel it moving. The tour was a little long, yet nice. I enjoyed the company and laughter of our group. I enjoyed laughing, talking and flirting with the employees. Big Shout out to Germantown United Methodist Church. Big Thank you to Mrs. Ellen. To the writing group, you know I love u folk.

Veyshon Hall

Looking straight ahead I put one foot in front of the other. I can do this! Entering through the sliding doors, terror runs through my mind. Oh! "You can't sit there. That's Mrs. Ellen's seat."

With a warning beep, a slight swooshing noise, and clinking noises of the machinery we're off. My breath catches in my throat. My fear is all around me. Please nobody move! I look across at another passenger! Lord help me! I catch a glimpse of the landscape around us and the drop! Lord don't let us die! My heart drops as far as that river bottom. My eyes return quickly to the floor. Someone, I'm not sure who, says, "We're almost there!" I look up again, we're pulling into the station! Praise God! I made it! I didn't fall! I didn't die! Tears well up in my eyes!

Cynthia Crawford

Well, first we got our T-shirts. We all was on time and everybody was just reading the backs of everybody's shirts. It was nice to see everybody so happy and laughing.

Next, we went to eat at a restaurant. I loved the decor—all of it, the lanterns, chairs, and the tables! It was full of people and it was funny when Mrs. Ellen got up and helped out—started carrying drinks and food out on a tray. She did a GREAT JOB! The lady at the restaurant went around and kissed everybody on the head before we ate. That was strange but nice! Some of us went out to smoke; Veyshon was standing there and a bug landed on her and she jumped so fast, it was so funny. We met some Navy guys from out of town. Ok, then we left and went to the museum!

It was fun to walk through not knowing what's around the corner and to feel like we was moving. That was neat! And most funniest was watching Cynthia and Robbin on the monorail going over to Mud Island. They looked like they was going to pass out, but coming back both of them was fine. Then we ended it and came home. All in all, I had a great time on my first outing with my writing class.

Thanks again!

Rhonda Lay

My perfect meal is fried chicken, salad with rolls with butter and desert. Fried chicken, really all chicken prepared any way. I can eat it every day. At one point in my life, I ate chicken daily. Now I'm branching out into different foods. But chicken is still my favorite. And always will be. Thank God for food. We went on a trip downtown to a restaurant that had fried chicken, green beans, mac and cheese with bread and sweet tea. Which was perfect for me because I love chicken. Thanks Germantown Methodist!

Donna Connie

Going out into the community and helping from the Door of Hope. I did and went to Idelwild Church and they let me stand where the candles are and do a church service one evening for them. That was the going out from the Door of Hope to affect the community.

William L. Hogan, Jr.

I often sit and stare out my window. The pale blue sky and drifting white, puffy clouds invoke a feeling of vague serenity. Cars travel back and forth with the muted tone of busy engines. A bird flies by. It's a mockingbird. Those dauntless creatures that will violently defend their nest. I've been pecked in the head by them a few times for being too close.

Here and now the natural blends in perfect harmony with the manmade. The huge parking garage of a hospital strikes a stark pose against the blue sky. While the lofty green trees accents this glorious canvas of color and light. Of movement and stillness. Of shadow and substance.

Of life in its fullest rewards. At these peaceful moments I am. I am here and now. I exist. Love flows like a gentle stream. Through the shadowy labyrinths of lucid mind I was here and now from the beginning of time. A vibrant atom in the mind of God. I danced to the music of creation then glowed like a firefly on a summer night. I am. I am here and now. In the fertile womb of space and time. I have no regrets or futile hopes. Just pleasant moment and misty dreams.

The leaves rustle as they dance with the autumn breeze. The song of life plays a symphony in my soul. Electric colors embrace the sky. The sunrise of life breaks the horizon, and I slumber away in lucid calm.

I am. I am here and now. Everything before me exists in the mind of god. And I am a shadow of his infinite will. So imperfect but yet sublime I am, I am here and now.

Tommy Payne

It's nice to have a safe place to live and be close to stores. Looking forward to having my own home here in Memphis. I am one of the lucky few.

Master Major Joshua Williams

The last thing at night before I go to sleep is to ask myself if I followed up on my plans for that day, was I pleased, and did I complete them. If I completed them, I say "Thank God."And I start planning my next move for the next day.

In the morning when I wake, I hit the floor running, after I thank God for my waking up. I get me a cup of mud, check the news and weather, maybe eat a small breakfast, get suited and booted and hit the road for another great day.

Leroy Scott

There is a lot to talk about the Civil Rights Museum—the education of the movement; from the 1700s to present day! I am so interested in the sacrifice each individual person put in carrying a message of equality and justice! The museum itself is so heart felt! It really touches my soul to be there in the exhibits, to feel the Spirit of each person that is connected to the movement. I was so touched to be in the 2nd part across the street from the hotel. Where they say the shot was fired! And to go into the mind of someone who would want to take a human life from someone who is on earth to carry a message of good-will and peace for all! And to try to stop a movement! I am so glad the museum is there with the set-up, so we won't forget—the struggles the people went through to get the rights we have and keep them in place for the next generation and the world to see and use in everyday life! God bless the ones before and the ones to come after! Keep the movement moving for a better world!

Roderick Baldwin

RODERICK BALDWIN

I am Roderick Baldwin. I was born in Tunica, Mississippi. The most important event of my childhood was moving to Memphis in 1967. My family is still in Tunica and elsewhere. I was first without a place to live in 1994. My homelessness was caused by drug-alcohol abuse and not being responsible; it lasted ten years. I got out of homelessness when I went to transitional housing. I heard about the Door of Hope and started coming to writing group in 2007. At the time I had an apartment. I kept coming to writing group because it was being part of something that made a difference in people's lives. The thing I enjoy most about writing group is being able to share my experience and hopes and dreams—and have an opportunity to discuss what's going on in life. The hardest thing for me in writing group is not being afraid to share my true feelings. If someone thinks homeless folks in a writing group is strange, I'd say don't judge them. I'd advise others starting a writing group to be honest and open-minded. The most important event of my adult life has been recreating my life and growing spiritually and having a willingness to help people—unconditionally.

It takes a lot of humility to do good; but if a person wants to live differently, a person has to grow by their own choices, being God-like.

DEDICATION

I would like to dedicate this book or writings to Verna Hailey Baldwin (Mother). Her motherhood has helped me survive the ups and downs of life. Her Spirit I know is in me, being her son. She loved me so much that she instored the morals and values I stand by today—to respect people and treat people the way you want to be treated. There are so many memories I hold onto that give me a peace and happiness in my life. I know being her son, I did have my days where she worried about me because of some attitude and behavior issues. Her love and caring often unseen has helped me make it through the hardest of times. I am very thankful God gave me a mother like I had—very Spiritual and very tough living. Without her love, I don't think I would be in the place I am in today. I am truly blessed. Thank you Momma. with love, your son.

CHAPTER 9
WRITING

From the beginning of my life there has been a voice. It starts with putting words together or the proper ones that come together to send a message of what you want a person or persons to listen to. We as people do communicate though our voice of opinion. We will not agree all the time; hopeful we can come to a understanding of the message we are trying to say. Like I said, everybody has a opinion—good or not so good. We have so many voices in the world. We the people who write about a personal opinion, we have dialogue to hopefully come to a peaceful solution. But there are people in the world who has a voice that is not a positive one. But do we learn from each other's voice; or we can use it to hurt or make trouble for others. So the key is good communication to keep the peace.

So everybody has a voice, but it's up to the individual what comes out of one's mouth.

Roderick Baldwin

Our writing room is painted beige. We have a bulletin board and a calendar on the wall. On the other side we have a plaque that says Live, Laugh & Love. We also have a ceiling fan. It's kind of small and cozy. It has a long table in the middle with a red and white picnic tablecloth on it. It has 2 medium square tables. One has a green picnic tablecloth, the other has a blue picnic tablecloth with flowers on them. We have two round tables. One has a green tablecloth, the other has a blue tablecloth. It's cool and comfortable from the air conditioner blowing. It smells a little like coffee when I first get here. It's relatively quiet when we are writing. Before class we have lunch. I still have a slight aftertaste in my mouth from lunch.

Latasha Jackson

A time to catch up with each other. Find out about up and coming events. Share our hardships, triumphs and love we have experienced. Show pictures, show off, poke fun at. We talk, we read, learn, or say nothing at all. This is our safe place, we exhale and breathe deeply. We have peace of mind. There is no punishment for speaking or not speaking . . .

What is this glorious place that only the homeless can find? It's the Writers Group, silly, located on N.Bellevue that is . . .

Veyshon Hall

Rainy days, picnics at camp, and being a writer. Being together. This is what makes me happy.

Anthony Johnston

Miss Ellen is a good worker of people in her class. She has a writing group and she comes every Wednesday and gets up with her material the people of the Door of Hope. She is writing for her job. We would not have a writing group if it was not her. She comes every week and gets us to write. I am happy she gets with us every week and do writings. I have experienced going to the Commercial Appeal Newspaper company and after a good amount of time she does things with us. She is making a book in which every week she gets written material from us and puts it in the book. I can really get my mind open in this group and have good writing and I turn them in. I get a lot of enjoyment out of writing for Miss Ellen. I think she is great.

William L. Hogan, Jr.

Today in writing class Ellen wants us to do some free writing whatever that is and it's driving me so crazy and it's funny and frightening at the same time. It is also very interesting. It's like blanking out and waking up at the same time. In other words very challenging and mysterious. For some reason I think this practice is being used to psycho-evaluate mixed up people. And it seems to be a good tool.

Leroy Scott

I like when people listen because you can express your feeling and tell them how you feel about the situation or things they need to know and show and tell them how you care about a situation. The Bible tells you when God made the world he spoke it and whenever you ask in his name he will hear you. So it's very important to speak your voice. Long time ago somebody told me you didn't have no voice, it just made me determined to go forward in life no matter what people say about you. Just keep pushing in life.

Robbin K

Having a weekly writing group is most important to me because it gives me something to look forward to. It's a sense of belonging. People do notice when I have missed a week and they say they missed me. It's like a family similar to my church. I get an opportunity to put my words, thoughts, and feelings out there. I also get to hear other members writings too. We get to bounce ideas off of each other so that each individual has a chance to improve and grow as a writer. It's exhilarating to see people's reaction to what I have written. And then seeing it published and being paid is like icing on the cake. Public reading is to me the same as reading out loud in weekly group. The excitement of ohhs and ahhs as well as the applause at the end. Field trips give you additional life experiences to add to your repertoire of writing material. Finally, there's the Annual Writers Retreat, which I thoroughly enjoyed. This year was my first year so I think that is why it was last on my list. I believe as time passes and if God wills me to be a part of the Retreat in the coming years, it will move up on my list.

Cynthia Crawford

The writers retreat was a meeting that was well set up. People were talking when they needed to make a point. They would come out and speak on what they had for us out of their information. I did get some opportunities to talk. We read from papers that were put together. It had subjects from what we got in the writing class. We took a break and then we had lunch and got back to the group.

William L. Hogan, Jr.

I really like the weekly writers group because I get to sort out my ideas and thoughts and write them down. I also like The Advocate a lot because I get to get my writings published and I get paid. I enjoy being a part of the writers retreat because we get a chance to get with other writers, professionals and non-professionals, to learn and express our ideas and share our experiences. I like our outings with our partners a lot also. I get a little nervous at our public readings. Having a guest is always nice.

Latasha Jackson

Writing, to me, is a creative gift. It represents a special talent or ability to transfer thoughts into words then put these words on paper in a constructive intelligible manner.

Writing can be stylistic according to the particular flavor and scope of the writer. It is easy to tell a book written by James Michener from a book written by Ian Fleming. An Ernest Hemingway novel from a play written by Shakespeare.

The written words are reflections of the author's inner being. I am somewhat a very exacting and focused, but poetic person. I could probably write a whole book about taking a bath. This does not necessarily make me a good writer. Too many details without coming to a definite point. The poetic side of my nature sort of compensates for many microscopic details. The book of bathing would not really be that boring.

The author pours himself into the characters he depicts in his works. A writer must also have a broad knowledge of human nature and the entire scope of human personalities. The writer must be also an astrologist of a sort if he or she is a fiction writer. I will spare you further details by saying, in closing, a writer must be, on top of every thing else, a well read person.

Tommy Payne

If? A great and powerful word. Whether posed as a question or a statement. If I had only done this or that? If I do this or that? Weigh out the good and the bad.

Writing to me is all good. It's an art all its own. Writing is like my therapy. Express yourself! It's educational, physical, and spiritual even.

So often there are things I think, that I will never say. The same is true with writing. I write things I would never say. So take a load off. Grab a pen, some paper, nouns, verbs, and adjectives. Just like reading a good book, you never know just where writing will take you!

The only bad thing I associate with writing is if it is done to intentionally hurt, embarrass, or slander someone.

Writing, just do it!

Cynthia Crawford

If I was to have a picture taken for the newspaper I would like for it to be a group picture with the writing class to impress upon the people of Memphis and the world the importance of reading and writing. I think it is so beneficial and just a great feeling. It is a feeling that you are steadily growing mentally.

Leroy Scott

As a little girl my sister and brothers used to poke and make fun of me. But I got over it and grew older and wiser. I wish very much that my sister and brother could be here for my reading because I miss them so much. That would make them proud of me to see that I am doing good and positive things.

Jacqueline Crowder

I wish my mother could have heard me do the public reading. She's been dead since 1979. She was always my favorite person and I remember as a young boy I would always try to make As in school so she could be proud of me. She had high hopes for me. I was so smart and charming. She thought I would one day be a doctor or a lawyer.

Well, things didn't turn out that way. But for what I've done in writing class and at Door of Hope, I'm sure she would be proud of me still.

Tommy Payne

When I hear a writing being read by someone else and it's mine, I am glad that this work of mine is doing a job. I have so much more to write about in here. I want you to be patient with me to put something together from thinking and some things in my folder.

William L. Hogan, Jr.

For one of the first times, I am experiencing writer's block at this moment. Poems aren't my best stroke. I'm filled with a lot of topics but nothing comes through so I wish to everyone a great day of writing!

Now as far as the poem goes:

If music is my life, today is the blues and my instrument is the trumpet. The way my life feels is smooth. Right now my color is brown and last but not least is the way I feel when I leave the Door of Hope—I feel like a big football player.

Leroy Scott

Here is the paper.
Here is the pencil.
Where are the words?
Perhaps somewhere in my mind.
Perhaps trapped in time.
Where are they?
I just can't grasp them today.
Some day maybe they will find a way back.
Hey, I think I am getting the knack.
Pencil brushes over the paper so smoothly.
The words are coming more now easily.

Ta da! Writer's block be gone.
Cynthia Crawford Writer and Author Extraordinaire is back.
And …. Poof ! There went my words again.
Straight out the door.

             Cynthia Crawford

I'm not really sure what I'm feeling in this space of time. Am I sad, mad, glad, bored, depressed or what? My emotions are all over the place. I feel really strange, my body is tired like I'm sleepy, my mind is numb. My spirit, kinda dragging. Whatever this mess is I'm going through, I'm not really worried about it. This too shall pass and all that good stuff. Today is definitely a whatever day, but don't get it all twisted or you may get twisted.

             Veyshon Hall

I was never expecting to earn any money from writing class. The news that we would be paid came as a very good surprise. I enjoy writing very much. Getting paid for it doubled my enjoyment. It is something to look forward to even though it isn't very much. But—it's the thought that counts. I feel more professional by getting a small but gracious sum of cash for my writing.

             Tommy Payne

I am very honored to be in this group.
I have a good taste for writing and getting attention.
The Door of Hope opens that door I say.
I write from ideals, my writing and stories get through the door. I hope we have it here writing and stories class in the Door of Hope a long time, three years more, all that you get out of a story is thinking a long time.
Thank you.
I hope I make stories again and again for the Door of Hope.

             William L. Hogan, Jr.

I've attended the Door of Hope writing class for almost five years.

During this time I have felt a deep sense of purpose and useful knowledge that could be shared with other people. My opinions, thoughts, etc., have been well received by the readers of the Advocate, our monthly newsletter.

My writing ability is not that perfect. I can be opinionated, judgmental, and callous when provoked by something I feel isn't right socially or morally. I was surprised to find that many people feel the same way I do but just don't have the nerve to say it. I guess I have the gall to say what many would like to say and that's a good purpose for my life. The writing group has given me an opportunity to reach others on a massive scale and project my identity.

Many times the results of my writings are inspirational. I have a tendency to hit nails on the head and get to the bottom line with the force of a sledge hammer. I just don't sugarcoat issues.

All in all I have learned to respect my own talents, and not disrespect the talents of others. Much success for our writing group! Hopefully I can be successful, too!

Tommy Payne

I have been writing now for a few years and one thing that I have noticed is that when you are writing it is like you are bleeding. I mean your soul just rolls out and it is as if you are bleeding, like a transfusion, a good one, especially when you make a great point.

Leroy Scott

I have always had a desire to write cards for Hallmark. I have always been able to find a card that fit the occasion perfectly.

I have been writing poems since I was a small child. They just pop into my head. It is a gift from God. I can write about anything in a matter of minutes. My poems touch the heart; they fit the moment or event.

There is one area I feel that Hallmark does not address. That is the inmates and their families. I would like to write in that area and others as well. Below is a sample of a poem for the moment . . .

Hallmark has the best greetings,

Poems and sonnets that touch your inner being.

Everyone can find a card that fits best,

Because Hallmark standards are truly above the rest.

I know I'll write greetings for them on day,

Cause God just works that way . . .

Veyshon Hall

I think the way to get started with a topic is to think it. I look at my paper and then think of a topic and the topic just comes up naturally. Really, if you think up a topic you can write with imagination. Think back in your past on a picture you have in mind and first write a title, this will be your topic. Start writing a paper. Think a little, wait and look up out of your notes and you will get a topic.

One of my favorite topics is to come to the class and it's when I am writing up the paper and finding myself watching the woodwork in the house. My favorite piece of the woodwork is the doorframe. I find myself wanting to be at the top of that woodwork piece feeling close to its inches. Another topic is get the pages that I made and put together papers in my folder.

William L. Hogan, Jr.

Words are so powerful in this world and the hereafter. Words can build up or tear down. They can help the writer relieve stress, hurt, and pent up energy. As the Bible says, "Power of life and death is in the tongue."

Words can teach the listener and heal the writer. Have you ever woke up not feeling good, and said, "I'm so tired and depressed." Then looked back wondering, "Why am I so tired and depressed?"

If you wake every morning no matter what and in Jesus Christ's name speak power, blessings, and healing and strength over your day, I promise it will change your life. For the better!

Cynthia Crawford

I think we should use public money to support the arts because it's important to keep the arts. It gives people an opportunity to express their creative sides. It's important to keep the arts so that our lives won't be boring. If we didn't have the arts we might not be able to alleviate some of our stress. It's bad enough to lose your job, but you might be able to go see an opera or visit the museum or paint a picture to have some sense of normalcy.

Latasha Jackson

Stop turning away when you hear my voice because I am not the smartest person in the world, but you can or may hear something that you can learn from me. I know the deaf can not hear but you can let this be a lesson to learn.

Jacqueline Crowder

JACQUELINE CROWDER

I was born in Memphis in Orange Mound. I liked going to school, being around children my age, field trips, and being around my hero, my mom. Most of my family has passed, except for my nieces. I was seventeen years old the first time I was without a place to stay. My family didn't want me to be around them. I was with a wrong group of people in my life. I was homeless three to four months that time, then another six months, then it started getting deeper. I was a mother while I was homeless. Then I started growing up. I began by myself, in and out of shelters. I heard about the Door of Hope when I went into Living for Christ. June Averyt came into my life in 2009. I've been coming to the writing group since about that time.

I kept coming to writing group because it's helping show me some things I can speak out on and didn't get hurt. Each time I spoke it led to me feeling better on the inside. I can open up. What I like most about writing group is it makes me part of a family. The hardest thing is speaking out, getting your thoughts together. It's confusing a little bit. Once I get it together, I feel good on the inside. My favorite topic is homelessness.

To those who think homeless folks in a writing group is odd, I'd say they ain't never been through it like we have. I'd tell others starting a writing group to be good at what you write—be honest with yourself, whatever it comes out to be.

I have four children and two grandchildren.

DEDICATION

I would like to dedicate the Door of Hope book to my children, JaDonna, Latoya, Darrian, and Demario.

PART III
WHO WE ARE NOW

CHAPTER 10
DAY-TO-DAY UNFOLDING

Yesterday was very interesting for me. My day started out with June and I arguing about my room not being vacuumed out. You see my room is to be an example of the Door of Hope and all it stands for so you know it has to be right and I totally agree. I hadn't been feeling good lately and my chores show it. So I had to suck it up and get back on the stick. So after about ten good minutes of getting roasted we were off to my doctor's appointment.

Once at the doctor's office the nurse did her regular routine. She weighed me, checked blood pressure, did a blood culture and took my temp. The doctor came in and asked how I was doing and I told him. I had some aches and he prescribed me another drug for acid reflux and pain. He gave me another appointment and told me to have a great day.

Having had a full day already I chose to take a nap. When I woke I vacuumed my room and June's office. She was so pleased as was I. After that she took me to the pharmacy to pick up my prescription. I got back and went to the store where I bought some tuna fish and bass for dinner, which I so richly enjoyed. I went over to some friends' house where two guys got into a bad misunderstanding and started to fight so I left and came home to call it a full day.

Leroy Scott

My best memory of 2012 was being with a friend. What made it special was, we met again at the Door of Hope. I first saw her in the park here in Memphis and we got along good. She had asked me for

$10 that morning for gas and food. You see, we were both homeless, though not for the same reasons. We became friends. We go out to eat now and go shopping. She is my special friend that I can call.

Master Major Joshua Williams

A tug of the cord signals the driver to stop at the next bus top. A lady's pre-recorded voice announces, "Stop Requested." I hop off the MATA bus and cautiously cross over Elvis Presley Blvd. Not always an easy task with the myriad of traffic that flows north and south on the boulevard 24/7. Then I head east to my apartment. As I ascend the hill I am greeted by smells of stagnant water and carcasses of stray animals. Continuing further, I pass potholes, abandoned houses, and over-grown trees, bushes and weeds. I am comforted by the smell of sweet Wisteria as I walk. Looking ahead, I see the usual security personnel. I greet them with a smile, "Good evening, officers." To which they reply, "Hey, Ms. Crawford—how you doing?" "Good, good," I answer. Turning left down the first driveway in the apartment community, I am accosted by four of the neighborhood children. They are hugging me, saying hellos, and asking like twenty questions at a time. "Where you go today?" "How you feeling?" "You got any candy?" "You got a dollar, Ms. C.C.?" "You gonna sit on the porch with us again?" Like I said, the questions seem endless. I reply, "I'll be out in a few minutes, kids." Arriving home I change into some cooler, more comfy clothes. Retrieving my lawn chair, I place it on my front porch. When I re-enter my apartment, I grab a cold glass of tea, some cigarettes, and a good book. On an average day I have 15-30 minutes of quiet time to meditate and read. But on a very good day I may have one or multiple hours of peace on my front porch sanctuary. A lot of neighborhood kids have taken a liking to me. Conversations about their schools, families, and everyday events are precious to me. There is just too much negativity in this world today. So it's important to me when I touch these young lives to show them positivity, respect for self and others, and especially God's love. Once I am alone again in the peace and quiet, I sit back. I take a deep calming breath and stare into the heavens. The sky is so beautiful today. It looks like a crystal blue with an army of fluffy cotton clouds. Looking at the various birds soaring, diving and almost dancing in the sky, I quickly run back inside and fetch some bread. Outside sitting in my lawn chair once again, I begin breaking off pieces of the bread and throw it to the birds, laughing as they seem to fight for the bigger pieces. Now that is my Front Porch Sanctuary.

Cynthia Crawford

Baking cookies is so much fun.
Making batches for everyone.
The holiday is near
And we love spreading cheer.
We're covered in flour from head to toe.
We've made 500, but need to make more.
Then there are several rapid flashes.
We blink and stare and laugh out loud.
For Heaven's sake, could it be?
Someone has taken a picture of you and me.

Veyshon Hall

Yesterday I spent almost a whole day planting and watering garden vegetables. For a long time I was thinking about the miracles that god blesses us with. How a tiny seed grows into an edible plant that nourishes our existence.

Yesterday I thought about the nature of god. Was god an active force that created all things known to man or just another force of nature that follows an oblivious pattern of being.

Yesterday I began to paint my picture of a matador killing a bull. The matador is an extremely graceful acrobat. But I also questioned the humanity involved in killing animals for sport and how my painting would convey both aspects of the contest between man and beast.

Tommy Payne

Yesterday when we were planting sweet potatoes and other plants I just happened to notice the freshly planted bulbs that Ellen had planted. They had sprung up seemingly overnight and I was really surprised. She had been so doubtful about if they were going to make it and here they were outgrowing everything.

Strangely about a month ago I had planted some tomatoes and okra and they had grown a little bit but nothing like the flowers Ellen had planted. Which led me to form the opinion that flowers grow faster than vegetables or that her prep was better than mine.

Leroy Scott

When I think of summer food, I think of food that is refreshing on a hot day. Lemonade, watermelon, ice cream cones, a nice bottle of frozen bottled water. These are the things that are great on a summer day.

Donna Connie

I try hard not to be afraid of the dark. I learned that putting the covers over my face would help me to forget about it. Then I would say my prayers over and over until I fall asleep.

Jacqueline Crowder

My mornings are bright and OK. My days are better than usual because I walk. I hear stories on the radio and I enjoy time I spend alone. I read books and magazines. I try to learn something every day. This is mostly a every day thing, and I rest a lot. Reading leads us here to there and tells us how to set up our life and to be generous.

Anthony Johnston

I am a person that gets nervous when I am visiting the doctor. The nervous part starts with me when I go to a doctor appointment and have to be nervous when I am waiting to be seen by the doctor. The waiting makes me nervous.

William L. Hogan, Jr.

I get as nervous as a cat on steroids crossing the street. Even at red lights.

About two years ago an elderly lady drove across the median at Poplar near Bellevue. Paramedics said I was about 6 inches from death. I leapt backwards trying to avoid her and she only hit the lower part of my left leg. If she had hit me directly, I would have been a D.O.A. I have fourteen pins in my lower leg and ankle as a result of the near death event. My left hand is terribly scarred and I get jittery crossing the street.

On top of all this drama I was given a citation for making an improper crossing. As if I should walk two blocks to the nearest red light to cross the street.

Lawyers dropped my suit. They couldn't find my only witness. I come out of all this trauma penniless. I learned only a good lesson. Never trust a motorist to do the right thing.

But all thanks to god. I am still alive. That's what I am grateful for. Not a huge settlement.

Tommy Payne

I was just recently in the hospital for a hernia operation and it scared me to death. I had a hernia the size of a 5 or 6 month baby. I really looked pregnant when I looked in the mirror.

So one Friday night I was getting ready to retire for the night and I got one of the toughest stomach aches in my life. The pressure was immense. I thought my stomach was going to burst open. So I immediately dialed 911. When I got to the hospital I was hurting so bad I thought I was going to pass out. They took my blood pressure and it was 200 over some high number and I was praying for it to go down so that I could have something for pain. The next day they operated on me and removed the hernia. But for some reason two days after the operation I went into respiratory distress which is not a day at the beach. They had to tie me up by my wrists and ankles and put a tube down my throat so I could breathe and I stayed that way for 10 days which was the 10 worst days of my life so far. That meant no food or drink, nothing but IV solution and medication.

Leroy Scott

I suffer from insomnia. A by-product of depression. Sleep is not easy for me. Sometimes I have to fight to go to sleep. I toss, I turn, I cross and uncross my legs. To be honest, my mind is strictly on falling to sleep. It comes as a welcome reward for my nightly struggle. But I do thank god for the blessing of sleep. Before sleeping pills were invented, not a good word but a handy one, insomnia often led to suicide. Can you imagine your body being dead and in need of rest but some chemical imbalance in your brain denies you the blessing of sleep? I thank god for scientists that had the knowledge to discover the chemicals in the brain that cause sleep. Of course, sleep is also spiritual. It arouses the sub-conscious to reach the psychic level of dreaming.

I thank god for this also.

Finally, my eyes close and I awaken to a brand new beginning. Refreshed and ready to carry on my missions for that day. Thanks to god and thanks to science, I feel blessed and nurtured then get on down the road.

Tommy Payne

My eyes pop open as I hear the thunder of four little feet coming down the hall. I roll over as my bedroom door swings open. Looking around, I am accosted by two little angels jumping on my bed. "Really?" I say because I'm really not ready for this day. "Mommy! Mommy! It's Christmas! Get up! Get up!"

"OK! I'm up!" I say as I reluctantly get out of bed. "OK! Girls go sit around the tree. I'm coming." I retrieve my Bible and head for the Christmas tree in our living room. You see, before any gifts are opened, we as a family sit around the tree to read the Christmas story. Out of the book of Luke in the "Holy Bible."

Then, sure enough, the ripping and tearing of wrapping paper. "Cool! Just what I wanted, Mom!" says my older daughter. Then my other daughter says, "How did you know? I guess you really do know everything, Momma!"

Cynthia Crawford

I love my family. Five members or more in one house, get Ready to Rumble! The members of my family stretch from Memphis to Germany. We constantly lose touch with one another. To know my kinfolk is to know the true meaning of selfishness. Hell, yeah I love my family. Not just because it's the right thing to do. Because I know, when it really matters and I need them the most, they put personal differences aside and it becomes a family affair.

Veyshon Hall

I am thankful for the gifts I already have. But learning to utilize them is something I must pray for. I am kind of lazy… Not physically lazy or mentally lazy… I'm always moving and thinking. I'm up by five a.m. arranging and rearranging stuff. Cleaning up my living quarters and thinking of things to write about. Ever so often I'll grab some paint brushes and start on a picture that will take a month or two to finish. Mine is a peculiar type of laziness. I am not very ambitious or self promoting. I settle down into daily routines and many times I get stuck in these routines.

But once I get started on a mission, I can go full force. Getting started is my main problem. The new year will hopefully give me more psychic energy to go forward and put all my efforts into going forward. Not just daily routines.

I like to meet people and share ideas. I was asked to do a lent service in church. I have sat there for four years like a wise ol' owl but I've never participated in the church liturgy. Except for Sunday School. I like to talk.

I hope to do more than talk in the new year…and put more effort into a creative self promotion.

Tommy Payne

One of the best gifts given to me was a bicycle lock chain that I needed so desperately and it was from the Door of Hope this past Christmas. I liked it so because I was broke and really needed it because someone had stole my favorite bike some months before.

Leroy Scott

It's good to have friends, ones you can talk to and play games with. Like Monopoly or school or being a banker because education is fun.

Anthony Johnston

The biggest gift I have is understanding. I try to understand others instead of paying no attention. It really amazes me the gift of writing that is in our writing class. The gift of 10 people living in a house and getting along. When I wake up in the morning, that is a gift for God, the most important gift of all. I receive gifts all the time. Breathing, eating, reading, writing—those are all great gifts to have. So thank God that you have them. I wish I had the gift of helping others. I don't have that the way I want it, but I'm working on that.

Donna Connie

DONNA CONNIE

I am Donna Connie.. I was born in Brooklyn. The most important event of my childhood was being born. I came to Memphis in 2002 when I was 27 years old. My family lives in Alabama. The most important event in my adult life has been getting off the streets.

I was first without a place to live in 2008. I had no income. I was homeless 2 months. I became homeless again, which lasted until 2012. I had children while I was homeless, but they didn't go with me. I got into housing in 2012. I heard about the Door of Hope through the Salvation Army. I started coming to writing group in June of 2012 when I was living at the Door of Hope. I kept coming to writing group because I loved the people in class. I most enjoy hearing others' stories. The hardest thing is writing more than one page. My favorite topic is homelessness. To those who think homeless folks in a writing group is strange, I'd say, "Try coming to class." If you are thinking about starting a writing group, I'd say, "Go for it." I want to add, Thank you Door of Hope—all the staff and people living there.

DEDICATION

Thanks, Door of Hope

CHAPTER 11
JUST US

Birthdays are great—they are another year you are here... when there are so many who are not here. So I am so blessed for every birthday I get. The birth of a baby is always a good thing...which is that baby's birthday.

Donna Connie

I am a woman with a lot of different sides. I am a mother of 5 kids. I used to be a wife. I am warm and caring. I am compassionate. I can be moody but I try to stay cheerful. I can also be mean when pushed too far. I am sometimes impatient. I like to sing. I miss not being able to ride my bike, not because I'm not able, but because I don't have one. I like to play music. I am someone who likes to go to amusement parks. Sometimes I like to be in a crowd. I sometimes like to be alone to meditate and spend time with God.

Latasha Jackson

Fast as the wind, sleek and unique. There is something soothing about a panther. Their smooth shiny fur gleams in the day and night. I don't know why I like them so much. At one time I wanted a panther tattoo. I still do, but God already had the final word on that. I would like to raise one from a baby, maybe that way he won't try to eat me when he grows up. Panther Power!

Veyshon Hall

The unknown, who knows where it will take me.
Large crowds, will they reject me.
Elevators and the dreaded heights, or maybe it is the fall.
Lord knows he will never find me on an airplane at all.
Talking in front of an audience, but I am getting better.
Don't forget the all important job interview to climb the ladder.
I also get nervous when conflict arises and tend to avoid it.
I HATE conflict! I see no point in it.
I LOVE to sing but I get nervous in front of others.
Stairs also make my heart skip a beat; if I fall I know I won't hover.
Catching a bus to a new place or maybe it is the thought of being lost.
I also find my nerves jumping when I am asking for help or assistance.
You know as I look back over this my smile brightens and my hopes go up. I guess I am normal after all.
Oh! Darn I'm nervous again because that didn't rhyme.

Cynthia Crawford

What makes me happy is the Holidays. People laughing and talking around Thanksgiving and Christmas. A smell of all the good food that is being prepared. Thank God he can make things happen for us to come together so we can enjoy ourselves, friends and family. May God bless us to see more holidays to come.

Jacqueline Crowder

I've been told I could argue with a wall! Well think about it; at least they don't talk back!

SMILE!!

Cynthia Crawford

The something I have done that no one else has done at Door of Hope is being a big warrior (you know, the military). I am one who dropped by after war and stayed five years. I am staying until the next song writing job. I just come and go, and like here at Door of Hope.

Master Major Joshua Williams

One of the things that I can do is that I can read a book in less than an hour depending on how many pages are in the book. For example, if there are 300 pages in the book, I can read it in 1 to 2 days depending on how much time I want to spend on reading it. The reason why I can read a book in a short period of time is that I can speed read.

Leroy Scott

I feel God gave me the gift of seeing someone from their insides. I can see what type of person someone is, or were. I know what their heart is like in other words. People generally laugh at me for this so I keep it to myself.

I would know if the person has a kind nature naturally or through pretense. I tend to just live in the reality of things and situations as they cross my path. I'm more at ease around those whose inside nature is naturally warm, loving, kind, caring. For I know that that's their true nature.

I try to speak and be kind to all, but I feel some people I come across is all about the outside appearance. And is cold and full of hate on the inside by the words they speak and the coldness of their eyes. Yes, that's how I see inside, through the eyes.

WJS

I think one of my assets is that I try to always have compassion for others. I try to be kind and caring. I always try to keep it real. I think I am strong mentally. I am somewhat creative. I try to be sensitive (especially to not be offensive to other people's feelings). I am hard-working. I put a lot of effort into doing things. I'm cheerful and fun-loving.

Latasha Jackson

I am just a simple guy who starts his day off by thanking God for another day. I am so humble and I am the kind of person who today tries not to think of himself! But to serve and give to others by listening, giving a kind word! Doing the work at the Door of Hope helps me not to forget where I come from! To share of one's self to others and help me to grow spiritually! I want to treat people the way I want to be treated! Having a positive attitude maybe helps someone else! I am learning a lot about myself through the men and women I associate with. Being here with the guests helps me be a better person in life! And to accept life on life's terms! It's an experience! I am thankful for the people in my life!

Roderick Baldwin

If I had to be an animal, I would want to be a tall animal like the giraffe and rule the zoo. It is in our nature to be tall and being like the giraffe would be tall enough. The tall thing stands as going and living the good life.

William L. Hogan, Jr.

It was a beautiful Wednesday morning at home. I stepped out my front door, stretched, then yawned. Looking around I noticed the usual flock of finches, robins, and mockingbirds congregating in the oak tree in my front yard. Quickly I ran back into the house to retrieve one or two of the biscuits from the batch I had slightly burned earlier.

"Was that her?" said Fred the finch.

"Of course. Is your eyesight getting that bad in your old age?" answered Freda the finch.

"Hey. Good morning my fellow fowls. What's the commotion all about?" said Mary the mockingbird as she approached.

"They're slobbering over the thought of that human bringing us more bread this morning," patronized Robbin the robin from the next branch over.

Fred tweeted loudly, "Hush, here she comes!"

I came out and the birds flew down to the ground, looking around then at me expectantly. One actually came within a few inches of my feet! It looked down at the ground and then back up at me. Again looked down at the ground then back up at me. It actually appeared to be begging like a puppy dog.

"Oh! How sweet!" I said. Then I proceeded to break little pieces of crumbs off the biscuits and throw them down. I noticed the one begging finch had stopped eating.

Suddenly, he looked up at me and said, "Nice burn job, lady!" and proceeded to eat.

Cynthia Crawford

To me a really weird food is sugar cane. You chew on the cane until all the juice is gone out then you throw it away. It feels like chewing on straw. Another weird food is a pomegranate. You bite the seed to get the juice and then spit out the seeds. I don't know why people want to waste money like that. The seeds are little, you barely get to taste the juice.

Latasha Jackson

I have a sister who gets together with a special group of girls. They were AKA sorority sisters. Some talk goes like, girls, why you wear green and blue, you need to wear pink and green. See, their colors are pink and green. Pink first, then green. I thought this was funny.

Master Major Joshua Williams

I really hate to wait on things. When I have to wait, I get anxious and depressed.

I get really impatient when I have to wait. I start worrying about if they are still working on my behalf. I sometimes start calling and worrying them and panicking, just so they can tell me to be patient. I get nervous and start pacing. Then I pray and get my nerves together and get a little more patience and wait some more.

Latasha Jackson

If I had to choose a band that I would play in, it would be a jazz band and I would be a tenor sax player. I remember John Coltrane, Jack McDuff, and Kenny Burell in the album they made called Blowing in the Breeze. Each member of the group had a certain place in the record. But I think John Coltrane was the best in his tenor sax riffs and melodies. Even though Jack McDuff was a virtuoso organist and Kenny Burell was great with the lead guitar, Coltrane seemed to outshine all of them. I could sit back and listen to him all day. I know it takes a lot of talent to play a saxophone. I could pretend to play his chords while dancing to his gentle, then turbulent, melodies. His wife Alice played piano and Zoat Sims played drums. All of them banded together until you could actually feel an autumn breeze a'blowin'. I don't even know how to hold a saxophone, let alone play one. But in my vicarious life, I am Coltrane.

Tommy Payne

Love
Sweet and Warm
Flowing, Feeling, Breathing
Touch Caressing Kissing Hugging
Caring

Leroy Scott

Psychiatric determinations just don't always show a person's true character. Or inner qualities. Anti-social people are usually introverted loners with a tendency to shy away from social activities and be paranoid of other people's motives. I must admit I have fallen into this category at many stages of my life but it hasn't been a permanent disposition. Just periodic mood swings. I am sure that most people have at one time or another felt the same way.

I can't see this as a "disorder," but just a part of being human. I guess what makes my condition kind of disorderly is that I can be totally reclusive on one hand - and extremely loquacious and outgoing on the other hand. I can be very happy. By myself. I have no real need for relatives and sometimes even friends. I think it was Great Garbo who made the famous statement, "I want to be alone" sometimes.

Perhaps she was anti-social too?

I love society. I love people and different cultures. Anti-social is a misnomer as far as I am concerned.

But sometimes I want to be alone.

To gather my thoughts and plan my next moves.

I think it was Sigmund Freud who said the only sane people on earth are mute, catatonic, schizophrenics. They say nothing, they hear nothing, they don't talk or react to any outside stimulus. They live in a perfect world of their own. Absolutely anti-social. I won't go this far, I'm positive, but sometimes. I just want to be alone.

Tommy Payne

Shades of the Mind
A great many colors dance through my mind,
but the words are hard to find.
Hues of yellow, pink and blue;
to Almighty God be true.
Now white and black,
I've got the knack.
We shall not forget brown, green, and gray;
defending our country is the soldier's way.
Orange, purple and red;
true love I thee wed.
What about rose, lilac and puce;
so many colors I can't refuse!

Cynthia Crawford

What Allergy?
Strawberries, peaches, plums,
blueberries, raspberries, nectarines too.
These are just a few of my favorite fruits.
I like them just a little past ripe.
That's when they're the juiciest, what a sight.
I do have just one problem though.
I'm allergic to any fruit with fuzz, you know.
My face gets itchy and my lips swell up.
I just can't help it, I gotta eat 'em up.
Fuzzy fruit, good to eat.
What allergy?

Veyshon Hall

I am happy to just be alive and experiencing the joys and sadnesses of life. I am happy that I am human. With human emotions and human frailties. I could have been a tadpole.

Tommy Payne

I love the beginning of fall. I always think of a new beginning or a fresh start. It's when the leaves on the trees change. I love the colors of fall. They always look so pretty. I like to take a picture standing in front of the colorful trees. It's like God painted a beautiful picture. Fall is when the weather gets cooler. I love those cool breezes blowing on me. It can be very pleasant. I really appreciate the cooler weather. Fall is when we get that extra hour to rest.

Latasha Jackson

I decided to write about me today. Most of the time I write about serious issues and give them a twist of humor. Today I feel out-of-sorts, off track. I feel downright tired. Tired of what? you ask. Tired of being sick, tired of my situation. Tired of smart people doing the stupidest things. Tired of having to start over again. Most of all, I'm tired of being sad and acting like I'm not! Yes, I'm very grateful for what I have and where I am. I'm wondering if I will ever be truly happy again. Not because of riches or things, just for the basic need of Peace of Mind!

Veyshon Hall

What I consider as being a special gift is that I have survived some very tragic and overwhelming events. Things that would have certainly destroyed a person not having a survivor's instinct, tuned to a fine point.

I was once psychoanalyzed as a man with a Rolls Royce mind living in a Volkswagen environment. He also said I could endure severe brain damage and still function as a normal person. Quite a gift, no doubt.

I utilized this gift in the most dire circumstances and nearing old age, I am still standing. Being analytical, creative, and never short for words that tries to make some good sense. This is a gift and nothing I studied or practiced.

We all have special gifts as members of the human race. I didn't recognize my gift for a long time. Taking myself for granted and utilizing my survival instincts in not always virtuous ways.

I simply refuse to go away. My experiences have only helped shape a unique character. I should be a bitter and cruel person. But through god's gift to me - I am endowed with compassion and understandings.

I also paint colorful pictures in words and oils.

My special gifts.

Tommy Payne

If I could meet someone from the past and present, I would like to meet Mother Teresa. I am just fascinated with her life story and her way of helping the poor. I would ask her what it is like to be a nun, even though I have met nuns before, but she is at the global level, and about all the places she went to. I would ask her what her journey had been like, what she liked, disliked about serving, and what her hopes for the future of the Catholic institution are, as well as for those whom she served.

Tamara Hendrix

TAMARA HENDRIX

I am Tamara Hendrix. I was born in Memphis, Tennessee. My family lives in Memphis, Chicago, and different places. The most important event of my childhood was getting a retainer on my teeth. The most important event of my adult life was having a child and being a mother.

I was first without a place to live in 2002 when I was 24 years old. I became homeless when I lost my jobs. I was homeless 3 months. I became homeless again for 2 months. My child was 5 years old. I heard about the Door of Hope through Miss June and got into housing at the Door of Hope in July of 2012. I started coming to writing group at the same time. I kept coming because it was interesting and fun. What I enjoy most is hearing different stories. The hardest thing is hearing stories of pain. My favorite topic is current events. To those who think homeless folks being in a writing group is strange, I'd say, "Don't knock it until you try it." If you are thinking about starting a writing group, I'd advise you to pace yourself. Keep God first.

DEDICATION

I would like to dedicate the Door of Hope book to my son, Darrell, who trusted his momma so much with his future that he let her go for a while so she would see God's plans for her. Not many children would understand the reason for separation or what I had to go through to get back to him, but he has understood. Never complaining about a new living situation, or that Momma won't be there to get him up for school every day like she used to, never crying except for the tears of joy when we have reunited. Thanks for sharing your mom with a wonderful organization such as the Door of Hope and its writing group. Without the Door of Hope and the love of my family, I could not have made it through these last couple of years. Thanks to my mom Annette and my cousin Danette—your support and love are worth more than gold. Thanks be to God for his mercy and another chance.

CHAPTER 12
MOMENTS THAT INSPIRE US

With my bag of chips in one hand and a bottle of Lipton Green Tea in the other I sit back in my recliner to enjoy a movie. For maybe the 100th time I watch "13 Going on 30."

It's a simple premise. It's based on a 13 year old girl wishing to be grown as many children and teens wish now a days. She is magically transformed into a 30 year old woman. At first she is confused and longing to remember her life. Then she soon sees how real and cruel this world can truly be. Then she thinks she got everything she ever wanted. Soon she comes to realize there is a price to all of it, and wishes to go back. One of the theme songs to the movie recites the line "When will you realize Vienna waits for you?" The inspiration I draw from that is to take everything one day at a time. You may not realize your dreams are right there if you take a second glance. You can't rush it along.

Cynthia Crawford

Take a deep breath and feel the air fill you up with life,
Arise and stand tall, walk gracefully into the light.
Cleanse your body while clearing your mind,
Dress for your day as this may be your last time.
The door is already open, walk boldly through,
You have been given a map, you know what to do.
Stay on the right path as best you can,
You have all the tools within your hands.

No matter where you have been, what you have done or said,
You can always begin again and start today over again.
                              Veyshon Hall

There is a comfort to getting back and feel and listen to the sounds of life. People's chattering and music in the background and those little sounds that you don't see. It is very interesting when you get and be quite, listen to the sounds of life; also there is the feeling and sounds of life! It is a wonderful make up that God created in man to feel and listen to sounds of life around us. There for a time, I took for granted these things of life; thank God, for the chance to wake-up and smell the coffee; what a wonderful thing of life.
                              Roderick Baldwin

I think that taking a time off for a situation of peace, you should go to a place by yourself after getting silence to have peace. If the country have many people, the people move to a place where peace is a found like this we know of. The president moves to settle race differences on the races being elected president a leader and social peace leader. Start with a group of people and deal with the beginning and then work an end-up situation and making a result from his leader place to the business they got going and then work with his group and ends up with making peace.

Sometimes this happens—a man will go constant and make his self fit or at alone for peace.
                              William L. Hogan, Jr.

I am very proud of Gabby. She has overcome a lot in her life. I heard a little of her story. She is doing so good. I am happy to see an African American young lady doing well for the U.S.A. The whole U.S.A. team is doing very well. I keep them in my prayers. Keep up the good work.
                              Donna Connie

My most inspiring thing that I experienced was our annual Christmas Feast. We had in excess of over 50-60 guests which was quite a bit for the Door of Hope to serve. We had guests from all over the city and helpers as well. After our feast we had our usual Christmas gift give-away to those who had previously signed up and to some who had not and as usual it was a great as ever and we closed the day with a great feeling of joy and peace and the hopes of a great Christmas and Happy New Year.

Leroy Scott

These Tender Moments
I wrote a love song –
For your ears only
Hope it will tell 'ya lover
How I feel
Life's so uncertain
It's such a gamble
It's an illusion
But it's oh – so real
And these tender moments
Won't last forever
Life is a symphony
Of pleasure and pain
I wanna' love you
Love you forever
But I'll drift away
And never see you again
Life's much too short
But oh so thrillin'
We never, ever seem
To have enough time
To catch a dream
To cast a shadow
To find that elusive
Peace of mind
And these tender moments

Won't last forever
Like flowers dancin'
In a springtime breeze
I wanna' love you
Love you forever
Thru endless summers
And autumn leaves
So let's do something
Something forbidden
Let's keep it hidden
Let's promise to never
Say a word
Let's fly to heaven
On wings of passion
Love's gentle whispers
That nobody heard
'Cause these tender moments
Won't last forever
Life is a symphony
Of pleasure and pain
I wanna' love ya'
Love you forever
But in my last breath
I'll never see you again.

Tommy Payne

In my imagination there is only love, harmony, peace and the occasional speed bump. The common cold is the worst illness we have. Violence is a curse word no one says or experiences. Homelessness, poverty and famine are not in the dictionary. Dying is a natural process, not a violent crime. Unemployment nonexistent and health insurance not necessary. Love is the national song and dance. I wouldn't be the superhero in this story, just a humble servant, like everybody else.

Veyshon Hall

My best Christmas ever was last year. I was helping the Salvation Army with the Angel Tree. I worked hard filling bags for little children, making the gifts fit the child. There is about 5000 bags to fill. Almost all of them get bikes, so you have to match the bike with the child. You don't want a girl to get a boy's bike or a boy to get a doll. Ya know!

It is a joy to me to do this every year because I don't get to be with my children and it's a blast to see the children when we come around the corner with these big bags and a bike. That's what it's all about, the joy on their faces makes me feel so happy! Sometimes I cry (it makes me). What a blessing! This is my 5th year doing this.

Rhonda Lay

One thing that inspired me, and that always inspires me around the holidays, is when people get into the holiday spirit. The way people start to think of other people. They try to make sure everyone has enough food at least for Christmas dinner. They try to help less fortunate children have clothes and toys. It really makes me feel like someone cares. I just wish the holiday spirit could last all year.

Latasha Jackson

Christmas is always a special time to me; it's the time to spend with family and friends. Also to reflect on the past and the present. It's also the time of gifts and also give thanks for all the blessings God has given us. A time to honor the Christ, who came to us from the Father. Christ came to give a message of hope and goodwill to Man and die for our sins so the holidays are special in my heart.

Roderick Baldwin

Over the Christmas holiday I found a lot of spiritual inspiration in a most magnificent sunrise.

I'm usually up by daybreak because of sleeping disorders. I'll get up about 4:30 a.m. and take a short hike to the hospital where I'll call my best friend and shoot the breeze.

This particular morning I saw at least 4 kinds of light.

The bottom half of the sky was an electric pale blue. In the middle of the clear skies was grey, ocher, lime colored clouds with brilliant auras of orange light to outline them. Then on top of the orange tinged clouds was a glorious clear sky with an off beige color.

I put this sunrise into my memory bank and made it a feature on a painting I donated to Door of Hope. Sunrises like this should always be painted. I did my best to capture it. I hope to see more sunrises like this. So inspirational!

Tommy Payne

I think about the time the President came to the Booker T. Washington High School. It was their graduation and he spoke very well about a lot of things that were very important to Memphis and that neighborhood. I have always liked the President for some reason. I was also very fortunate to be able to go to his inauguration in Washington DC. And it was one of the highlights of my life.

Leroy Scott

Music is my favorite thing in the world. It helps me when I am feeling bad, good, any mood. There is so much great music. I almost love it all. Some old music is as good as the new music. I favor rap & R&B the most. Some rap is like listening to my life. R&B is great for times when I am lonely. A lot of the great musicians died too soon. But their music lives on forever. I love hearing their voices. It helps when you are on an elevator or on hold on the telephone. This would be a sad world without music.

Donna Connie

Watching things grow gives me a great sense of being. The Door of Hope gardens give me the opportunity to be focused into a very pleasant state of mind. The patio is also a good place for me. I often sit with Leroy or Elvis and discuss the day's news stories and see who can make the wittiest remarks about them. It's a good place for old men to lean back and be just plain old men without many youthful impulses to speak of. I get a lot of joy by communicating with people as well as nature.

So between the patio and the gardens I can maintain serenity and not worry too much about my problems. And what has already happened in my life. Things I cannot change. I can change seeds into vegetables and flowers and people's opinions about many issues. Which is a great accomplishment.

Tommy Payne

What is peace—peace is a calmness—quietness in one's mental, spiritual and being in how a person feels about oneself or the decisions it makes and be ok with it. There are a lot of ways a person or anything on earth can be at peace: it can be in a place or the thing they are doing to make themselves feel good! In our everyday life being at peace of how the economy is run, the support of all government run agency, be at peace with what they do! Everybody can be at peace if they choose to be! Being in or at peace is God given! But not everybody is going to be at peace all the time! That's why people pray for peace and good will – because there are a lot of evil people out there who has no peace!

Roderick Baldwin

What makes me happy? Hmmm ... Let me think about it. Oh, I know, peace of mind. Notice I said peace, not a piece of my mind. I don't need many pieces of my mind to be happy. Being at peace means that my relationship with God is unshakable. It means that no matter what small or large issue I have, I trust God's deliverance. Sure, I will yell, scream, stomp, throw things or cry. I may even feel bad about it. God knows every little thing about me and will continue carrying me, guiding me and loving me. Peace of mind is a happy thing. Now if I could just remember where I put those pieces of my mind.

Veyshon Hall

I have to laugh. I think laughing is the most wanted thing in a person's life. Many times I was thinking of something to go laugh about and I got the feeling of it and thought up words and happenings to make myself laugh. I caught on to it in 2006. I can hear a person talk, he may talk to another person, and a smile come on to my face. I'll be around the house and I'll be waiting on something to come up to my ear and I'll go along with my day and wait and sooner or later I will laugh and smile. I'm tickled.

William L. Hogan, Jr.

The person I think was a leader to me is my late spiritual mother. I consider her a leader because she was bold and courageous. She had a beautiful spirit. She always made you feel like you were important. If she asked you to do something, you were glad to do what she asked. She was strong but gentle. She always had an encouraging word for you if you felt down. Everyone looked to her for guidance and advice. She inspired me to be the best I could be. She's not with us anymore, and I really miss her, but I am happy, because I know she's in a better place.

Latasha Jackson

I would like to tell my sister Vivian who died in October that I love her very deeply even though I didn't communicate with her as often as I should have. I had noticed her smoking a large amount of cigarettes for many years but never did I tell her the dangers of lung cancer from cigarette smoke. She listened to me on all issues and occasion and my influence on her was great. Why didn't I chide her about smoking? For some unknown reason I never did. Then she died a month ago from lung cancer. Of course it's not only caused by smoking cigarettes but by several reasons. But I'm sure that in her case it was from cigarettes. This makes me feel like I failed her as a loving brother. So if she can hear me, I'm so very sorry for not showing her enough love that could have perhaps saved her life. Vivian, I love you.

Tommy Payne

WJS

I am WJS. I was born in Georgia. The most important event in my childhood was vacation time, going out of town every summer. I moved to Memphis in 2005 when I was 43. My family lives in Memphis. I am a grandmother. The most important event of my adult life was rediscovering myself.

I was first without a place to live in 1996. I became homeless because my mother passed. I had sent my children to stay with their grandparents in Memphis and I lost interest in life. I was angry, hurt emotionally. I had a job but had to quit due to the death of my mother. I just didn't care anymore. I was homeless for 3 years. I became homeless again, for shorter periods of time. I was married while I was homeless, and I had children. I got into housing in May of 2012. A friend told me about the Door of Hope. I began coming to writing group in September of 2012. I was living at home then. I kept coming to writing group because I love writing. I really enjoy the group. What I like most is the people and being able to express myself through writing. The hardest thing is writing and speaking about past and present hurts and events. But it's good therapy to heal. My favorite writing topic is 18th century architecture, basically anything but love stories.

I'd tell those who think homeless folks in a writing group is strange, "Don't judge until you've experienced it." If you are thinking of starting a writing group, I'd advise you to be true to your beliefs.

DEDICATION

I'm dedicating this piece to all those who've been abused, mistreated, misplaced, and to those of us who feel alone and that there's no way out, in my effort to let them know they are not alone and there is hope. Thank you.

Sincerely felt,

WJS

CHAPTER 13
GOD IN OUR LIVES

God's dream from the world is that he had made communication with man. He would rule the world to be man's authority and be like a book to man's benefit. Look all into man's body condition and try to get far in healthy and draw a border having god's things on one side and man's on the other and describe to us if we serve him in worship and religion have his materials for us to go through. He keep an ear open to those who worship. He would go into detail and show us all his parts. You see, he is a set-up to come and take of him freely. He would give us the time. He is your secret company, yes, your feeling friend with a heart of your relative. If you ask me, he's our spare time savior, a communication.

William L. Hogan, Jr.

I call myself God's listener. Total strangers feel the need to talk to me about whatever is on their minds. People love to unburden themselves on me.

At first I didn't like hearing other people's garbage. I felt like a dumpsite. I would get angry and that would keep some people from talking to me but not others. I kept wondering why people always wanted to talk to me. One day, after a series of strange encounters, I realized that they needed to talk and I really needed to listen. They helped me to understand my life better and feel gratitude.

Since then I don't ask why. I just know that I am one of God's listeners. When it becomes too much, I take a break and talk to God and get back to work. Every now and then I get shell-shocked when someone calls me instead of 911 when their child is choking. I remain calm and tell them what to do and encourage them to call 911. Phew, another life saved.

Veyshon Hall

I trust and depend on God for shelter and food. I trust and depend on God to get me through my drug and alcohol addiction, and he delivered me. I trust and depend on God when I want to see my children. I pray about it then I get to see them. I trusted and depend on God and he helped me to recover from my homelessness.

Jacqueline Crowder

I can feel God all around me as I go through life. I wake up to a beautiful sunny day, there's God. I hear the birds' chirping, there's God. I pray for strength to make it through the day, there's God. I read the scriptures, there's God. I have a meal with family and friends, share in their joy and laughter, there's God. When someone makes a "good deed" gesture, like paying it forward, there's God. God can be everywhere, in every situation from something as simple as combing your hair to something massive as a tornado. God is watching, waiting for us to call him to help when he is needed. I may fall from grace sometimes but I know that God is always willing to pick me back up again to start over.

Tamara Hendrix

Ever since I was a kid, I've wondered why people dust under knick-knacks. Or sweep and mop behind doors or furniture. You know beside the obvious that they want it to be clean in their home. Guests rarely look behind furniture, knick-knacks, or doors. But now GOD is teaching me if I am faithful with the little that I do have, He will bless me with so much more. It's not about what you or I see, but what GOD sees. He sees and knows ALL. The Bible says what is done in the dark will be brought to light. He who puts him or herself first here on earth will be last in Heaven, and he who is last on earth will be first in Heaven.

Cynthia Crawford

It felt like it was the end of the world for me when I lost everything. I didn't know how I was going to make it through. God reminded me that he said that he would be with me always, and that he would never forsake me. I got caught up in anger and self-pity. God told me that this was not the end, but a new beginning. I never would have got through it without the help of the Lord.

Latasha Jackson

New Beginnings to me is like God opens up and introduces us to our new life (the newborn babies). I get a feeling of excitement for some and a feeling of sadness for the others. Some will be loved and taken great care of. Some will be abused and neglected and even killed. It always amazes me that the Lord giveth and he also taketh away and sometimes I have a problem diffusing the two. So I try to keep my head up and appreciate the good times and pray for understanding during the bad.

Leroy Scott

My life, under deep religious convictions, has changed drastically. Most of my life has been agnosticism. I did not believe that god played any active role in human lives. I depended upon my own mentality which was not always positive. I felt as if I was completely on my own in life. Without any guardian spirit to shape my destiny. Whatever became of me was the result of my own actions or inactions. I was a defeatist to a great extent. I didn't put forth much effort to change my circumstances. Which revolved around drugs, alcohol and numerous trips to jail.

Something finally struck me as a guardian spirit after some confrontations with death. I saw, finally, some purpose in my life: to write and paint pictures that are pretty good. To be a good speaker and share my knowledge from reading countless books on a variety of subjects.

Tommy Payne

I heard about Memphis through the voice of Jesus. I am following after him through obedience. Once I came here, he guided me and directed me to two shelters. Put me in an agency called the Door of Hope. They have given me hope, courage, guidance and help only you can image. When you focus on your life and image the things you can do on your inner strength through him that's a number one of gift that people can't take away from you.

Robbin K

I was reading in a magazine and it said how you can consider myself to be time. So for Christmas this year I got a watch and they say when you give something to God, God will give back to you. And it does come back in another way.

Anthony Johnston

I am exhausted! Baking, serving, cleaning and more. Just when I think I can relax, there's more to do. If you think I'm complaining, I am not! What I am doing is spreading God's love everywhere. Don't you know that serving is the best way to show God's love? Yeah, I'm tired, but I'm not going to stop until God brings me home. I love to help others, sometimes they get tired of me. That's OK, cause I'm going to keep loving them anyway!

Happy Thanksgiving!

Veyshon Hall

We as a people, or the ones that believe in Christianity, have been honoring the life of Jesus Christ; or the days or week that Jesus was ministering to the people and the different break-down, we as a people set up the religions. The interesting thing about it, we as a people no matter which religion you are, Jews, Catholics, Protestants, Baptist and other, do somehow honor Passover and Easter in some general way. There are some of the religions that have their own ways and traditions of Passover leading up to Easter. We in my family come from different religions. What we were as different people of how we honor Passover. You had the traditional Easter Egg Hunt or Lent or the other ways we as a people would go out and buy new clothes or eat certain foods or only would live a type of way that their religion has them to honor that. It is supposed to be a special time if you believe in the Lord Jesus Christ and he was the Son of God. But there are some of us in the world that don't believe a lot of people have died because of what we believe in. The sacrifices the true Believers had to put up with because of what they believed in. So this time of the year there are a lot of us who do come together in good will to show the true meaning of Passover and Easter. It's not all about the Easter Bunny, the kid's love it, what a tradition. We do have a lot to be thankful for because Jesus died for all our sins; no matter what religion you are. God Bless all of us in this time of honoring Passover.

Roderick Baldwin

The pain was unbearable. I wanted to die. I didn't know what to do or say or who to turn to. I cried and cried and cried. When there were no more tears and my soul felt empty, I thought, "I must be dying." Then peace, like I have never imagined, entered my soul. I began to feel beautiful and alive, worthy. "What's happening to me?

Am I dead?" I asked myself. A giggly voice answered me, "No, silly, you're having a reunion with God."

Veyshon Hall

If I could have God change one thing about human beings, it would be our inability to forgive. Forgiveness is so essential in our daily walk with the human race because one cannot move forward and produce healthy relationships without it. I can't say I love my brother or fellow man if I can't forgive him for something that happened years ago. Jesus teaches us to love one another as he has loved us, so we must forgive because he forgave us. From the politicians on up, we should learn to forgive to heal our nation's relations with other countries. There would be less school shootings, work-related shootings or mass-shootings if we could get people to forgive.

Tamara Hendrix

It's always nice to be surprised, especially when you get something that you weren't expecting like some surprise money, a gift you weren't expecting, or even a surprise visit from someone you haven't seen in a long time. I have walked out and picked up money off the ground a few times. It made me feel so good to get that unexpected surprise, especially when I was feeling a little down. It's like God saying I love you, cheer up.

Latasha Jackson

Our land, seas and air are being polluted. Animals are being abused and abandoned. Woman against woman, man against man. Killing has become a sport. Teaching hate has become part of parenting. The sadness and fear I feel for the world, my family, and self is crippling. I'm on guard everywhere I go, I trust no one. I have taught my children that everyone is suspect, including family. I cry about the hatred running rampant throughout the world. Children having children. Children killing children, their parents or themselves. Whatever happened to, "The Children are our future?" We are in big, big trouble.

So I wonder, is God crying too....?
                    Veyshon Hall

May it please the lord, I would like to ask your blessing upon our lives and our families. That we will continue to follow the right path and do right things to ourselves and to each other.

There are many things to be asked for in the world. But maybe the greatest blessing of all is inner peace and compassion, not at the least understanding of your lovingness.
                    Tommy Payne

May the Lord God bless everyone in the city of Memphis with love and compassion for his fellow man. May the Lord also bless everyone this year with a good job and a nice house. May the Lord bless the city to care as much about homeless people as they do about homeless animals. May the Lord bless everyone to have a peaceful New Year, as well as a healthy New Year. May the Lord bless everyone at the Door of Hope, financially also. May the Lord bless everyone that is expecting a financial blessing to get it this year. May the Lord bless the hungry everywhere with food. May the Lord bless the naked with clothes. May the Lord bless everyone to be thankful and grateful for each blessing he gives.
                    Latasha Jackson

The Bible says how God is all good, powerful, knowing, and love. The Bible also says how God made us in his image. So to me that means if he is all these things then so are we. No, I'm not saying that we are perfect, because we are not. I just know that God is not a liar. But we all have the ability to be good. God set us apart from all of his other creations by giving us free will. The ability to choose him. The ability to love. The ability to be powerful. The ability to learn and grow as well as the ability to make good choices. What we do with these abilities is our freedom of choice and free will. These choices we make is based on upbringing, education, resources, our diverse surroundings be it people or environment. As well as God's presence in our life. What will you choose today?

Cynthia Crawford

CYNTHIA CRAWFORD

I am Cynthia Crawford. I am known as C.C. by my close friends. I was born in Oakland, California. I was in Memphis in the early '80s and still call it home today. My family lives all over. I love travel, music, and being creative. I am also blessed to be the mother of 4 children, 2 beautiful daughters and 2 gorgeous sons.

I first was without a place to live when I was 19, in 2001. I became homeless because I had no income. I was homeless 5 months. I became homeless again, which lasted 2 years. I was a mother while I was homeless.

I got into housing in December of 2011. I learned about the Door of Hope from the Salvation Army. I began coming to writing group in June of 2011. At that time, I was sleeping in a shelter. I kept coming to the writing group because it felt like home, and it became like family.

What I most enjoy about writing group is being able to get my feelings on paper. It's like therapy and social life. The hardest thing is going over hurt feelings and speaking aloud about those hurtful feelings. My favorite writing topic is comedy. To those who think home-less folks being in a writing group is strange, I'd say, "Don't knock it 'til you try it." If you're thinking about starting a writing group, my advice would be, "Don't be afraid to be yourself."

DEDICATION

I wish to dedicate this book to my 4 blessings, Sierra, Selena, Angel and Anastacio. They have taught me what true love is, how to love myself, and how to appreciate the little things in life, and what is truly important.

PART IV
ADVICE, TIPS AND WISDOM

CHAPTER 14
HOW TO HELP THE HOMELESS

First of all, I believe if members of Faith-based communities actually got out and pounded the pavement to get to know the homeless people in our communities, we could tell them individually what we need.

Personally, I would like it if programs were started to train us on how to become stable and remain that way. Maybe set up some internships with area businesses to hire through these programs people off the street. Also, once we are working, set up bank accounts to save money, or at the very least have a 3rd party help us filter our paychecks to landlords and bill holders and we would have what's left. More technical/vocational training on specified trades would help to make us more employable.

Of course, more intensive Case Management is a must. You have to know each individual personally. Because if you just clump everyone together, some people are likely to fall through the cracks.

I have 4 children. They have been in foster care since 2009. I sincerely want to work and be independent. I can't force someone to hire me. I can't get into housing 'til my kids are actually with me. Like a Catch 22, I can't get my kids back 'til I have housing and employment.

Cynthia Crawford

To help the homeless is to be homeless for 2 weeks out here and see how you feel, and be treated like an outcast. People are looking for somebody to treat them with respect and dignity. Show them you care and not only say you are going to help them, but show them compassion and love and the support they need from you.

Here's some steps to guide and help the people and families while they are homeless:

First step is, show love and support.

Second step is, guide them to shelter and food.

Third step is, contact the family for support.

Fourth step is, help them with mental and disabilities.

Five step is, reassurance by giving them hope and respect about themselves.

Six step is, ask questions about how they became homeless.

Seven step is, direct them to agencies for help.

Eight step is, show them they can make it and be able to stand on their own.

Nine step is, churches or pastors need to support them for housing, food, and clothing.

Ten step is, Jesus wants us to live comforted on earth and to help one another and encourage each other in the body of Christ.

Robbin K

The first thing we need to do is to realize that it actually exists and that we are all a part of the Big Picture. I'm pretty sure that at one time or another we have had someone in our own family or a close friend who has been homeless and was going through a bad time.

The first thing I think Memphis should do is to stop harassing the homeless in the downtown area. I mean what would you do if you were broke and homeless? You would go somewhere where someone has something to offer. Basic common sense, people.

So, in closing, what I think Memphis could, would or should do is have lunch with the writers group one day so that we might put our heads together to come up with a common bond for this problem.

Leroy Scott

These are what I offer the homeless:
You may ask them for a good night sleep.
You may ask them for some good food to eat.
You may give them a change of clothes to put on.
Last one -
You can always give good advice.

Jacqueline Crowder

I hate to see people get taken advantage of. How can someone profit off another person's misfortune? Just make me understand: how can anyone with a conscience make a profit off the homeless? Homelessness shouldn't be a business. This is someone's life. How can someone profit from someone else's pain? If I had a place like that, I wouldn't charge people that have had a hardship. I would try to help them get back on their feet. I think it's wrong to use someone's misfortune to get gain. Maybe it wasn't meant for me to understand.

Latasha Jackson

A person can help homeless people by caring for them and housing and feeding them and getting them Social Security benefits, so they can make monthly payments and can take care of themselves.

When I was homeless I need a place to stay & benefits. The Door of Hope helped me with food and clothes.

Master Major Joshua Williams

As a person who was once homeless, I see that if the city and faith-based come together, they need to get with the nonprofit centers to help them see and learn what it takes to help. Sure, money does help, but how; stop the stereotyping or using the shelters as fronts to find lawbreakers; help people get educated on the rent; find the reason why they became homeless. They did mention financial counseling, parenting and relationship building. There needs to be a better way to connect the A&D programs along with the mental health outlets. There needs to be more tough-love! Having a person to attend church is not always the answer. Helping motivate them to do better through the resources!

Sure, there is a lot of individuals who don't have to be homeless. Some made bad choices in life; some had tragedies happen in the home or lost a job or have some type of mental disease. It's a matter of not keeping them homeless, but helping them see that there is hope. If they do the right thing and see what benefits they can get to help.

Sure, there is a lot of people who try to take advantage of the programs; or the people who really need the help. Sure, the shelters are good, but helping a person get to the resources like job training and education—there are a lot of homeless who need the help in the right way!

The thing is the faith-based need to practice what they preach in getting out in the community to help in helpful ways. It is not just giving a meal and clothes. From a person who was once homeless, having the willingness to help self and having support through the agencies—it can be done to end this madness!

Roderick Baldwin

So the mayor has decided to help the homeless . . . Where have you been all this time? We have been homeless for years. What about the programs already in place that are struggling? How can you help them to help us? How many new salaries did you have to pay for this collaboration? How many real homeless people have you interacted with on a personal level? While you and your team continue to live, eat, sleep and get paid well, we are still homeless. I didn't choose to be homeless. My health is the cause. I enjoyed working and being independent. Now I have no home, no health insurance, and a bleak future. Thank you again.

Veyshon Hall

I would like for the mayor to focus on a shelter so that the homeless people would not have to sleep on the streets. We need a shelter where we could take baths and put on clean clothes each and every day. Also a place where we could eat and sleep each night. It hurts so bad when we are not knowing where our next meal is going to come from, or where our next place to lay our head down is going to come from.

Jacqueline Crowder

I have no can opener..

I think the best thing you can do is treat them like humans. Maybe listen to them and don't think all homeless people are homeless because they want to be. Some people are even born into it without choice. Help someone if you can. You never know when it will be you. Treat others how you would like to be treated. So love everyone like God would want you to.

Donna Connie

Experiences in homelessness have made me more compassionate and understanding about the subject. I recognize the many issues that bring about homelessness. Most people that I met as a homeless person myself were either mentally ill or victims of drug and alcohol abuse. There are many other things that can create homelessness. But from my personal experiences mental illnesses and substances abuse are the foremost cause. It has been said that the jails are really mental institutions and rehab facilities now.

Care for the mentally ill has decreased to a great extent because of low funding and many restrictions about how much state funds can be used to treat the mentally ill. It's now about 14 days. No one can be treated in 14 days for severe forms of mental illness or drug addiction homelessness.

Much more funds are needed. The more this issue is raised the more society can contribute to care for the homeless.

Tommy Payne

If you are homeless, you should start at going to a church on Sunday and the preaching will give you a welcome of the church to get off the streets. This will make you feel at home that Sunday. Get the ball rolling to prepare yourself for the other days of the week. Figure rent. How much could you pay 2 weeks, 4 weeks, 5 weeks. You got a figure of 6 days remaining. Work, save up the asked for rent. Apply for disability if you have a disability or your social security check benefits.

Faith will see you through the door. Develop a sense of being through the door.

William L. Hogan, Jr.

I myself have given hot food, money, time and clothes, when they willingly accepted it. And for those who curse me out, or totally not take it because of pride, I say a prayer.

When I was homeless, it was trying on my mind and body. I experienced sleeping in parks, school buses, over at other people's houses when available. I used to shower at the hospitals. I worked day labor to support myself. Visited clothes closets. It was hard for me to ask someone I didn't know for a hand out. I was scared of becoming sick. Not being able to accomplish anything. Tired of people looking at me like I was the scum of the earth. I became homeless because my finances were taken from me, and I could not keep my payments for rent. So I had to vacate their premises. And didn't know where to turn to at that time, and didn't have family around me.

So there are many reasons why people are homeless. And it all cannot be blamed on drugs and alcohol, although that is one of its causes. As well as inflation, loss of jobs, death of a partner (financial) etc. So to this day, I treat them with the same respect I give to others. And how I would like to be treated.

WJS

If your house is destroyed in a tornado, the Government will give you a temporary house. Why can't they give the homeless a house until they can get one? People can help homeless people by helping them to find resources that will help them to get a home. They can help them find work. They can help them to get proper clothes to wear to a job interview. They can help homeless people by giving them a class in money management, or teaching them a skill so that they will be able to make a decent living.

Latasha Jackson

Surprise. Welcome to the jungle! Now that you're homeless, stay away from wayward people and troublemakers. Try very hard to meet people who are somewhat quiet and passive. Try to find a good church or a place that feeds homeless people and that has some kind of activities. And above all, try to get God in your life. Look for organizations that cater to the homeless. Try to create yourself a job collecting cans, doing yard work, washing cars, or doing any odd jobs.

See if you're able to qualify for Social Security and Food Stamps. Or any free health insurance. Make sure you have a proper ID or you will go to jail in a heartbeat and be denied benefits. And most of all be kind and patient and it'll take you a long way.

Leroy Scott

To the person who does not have a house, my advice I would give is to stay focused, keep warm, and if he or she ever gets or finds a house again, my advice is to tell this person not to make the same mistake again.

Anthony Johnston

To me the best thing you can do if you are homeless for the first time is to find someone you could get along with that's homeless and knows some places where you can get some help for food, clothes, shelter.

Churches are opening up more for the homeless people. Non-profit organizations are popping up more. But the main thing to do is search for the truth and have a lot of patience. For God is good all the time.

Leroy Scott

If you use a muscle or group of muscles to fight life with, you will operate in life much better, I experienced. Health is one needed part of the experience so get healthy, and you will go getting help from human service and find a spot just right for you to move in. Cover the body throughout the day and find your way into a job and/or time schedule of the downtown feed hall and this will do you good. And think of some songs and radio records, make your own songs. With physical health parts you will live a very long life. I am 49. Remember, thank God, be health wise and take it from me, William Hogan Jr., you will live a long life.

William L. Hogan, Jr.

Perhaps the greatest stigmas attached to homeless people is that they are irresponsible, lazy, untrustworthy, socially dysfunctional, and, for the most part, people to toss some pocket change at and then be avoided.

Broken families, broken homes, broken dreams, broken lives. Some people give up easily. They don't have the typical fortitude to rise above social conditions and personal tragedies. It is a rare individual who can rise from destitution or social neglect and function on a normal basis.

But is the government obligated to adopt a mandate of socialism and provide for those who for one reason or another cannot function in society? Or provide for themselves? Rewarding social misfits with free accommodations would be an insult to the hardworking. But discarding the mentally ill, drug addicted or socially neglected to die by the wayside would be an act of cruelty.

Each case must be looked at on an individual bases. But how do you separate the deserving from the freeloaders? By having a social economic and mental history available. Also by certifying the willingness of each client to undergo a social rehabilitation.

Tommy Payne

Every army started with one person's idea. Then the idea was shared and an army was born. Each one teach one. So, in saying that, any average Joe or Jane can help the homeless. Start by donating your time and experience. There is something that you have gone through that gave you some wisdom. Use that to help someone. Listen to a homeless person's story. Help them make phone calls. Read their mail for them, write a letter for them. Give them a smile. Every little good thing turns into big miracles. A blessing begins with one …..You!

Veyshon Hall

I have for one learned from homelessness to appreciate stuff, to manage my money, to respect people more, to pray for real, to wash my clothes better, to keep a clean house, to have more compassion for my fellow man. A deeper love for family & friends, a better use of my time, and a commitment to pay closer attention to my health & strength; to be a much better saver of money and other resources, and to keep God in my life much more.

Leroy Scott

I wish to be a part of a ministry one day to help homeless people.

I personally know how when homeless, your self image and esteem can go all the way down. I would give the men and women manicures, pedicures, makeovers, foot baths. I know these simple things can do wonders.

Everybody no matter the sex, age, race, body size, shape, religious background, or station in life deserves to feel like a million bucks. Like they have worth and value because EVERYBODY does.

Cynthia Crawford

CHAPTER 15
WHEN PEOPLE ASK YOU FOR MONEY

If someone comes up to you and asks you for money, I think you should give them at least 1 dollar. They are telling people not to give to panhandlers. They say they get help from agencies. You might need to go to the doctor, or you might be trying to go put in job applications. The agencies might give you 2 bus passes every 3 months. I guess if you have to go somewhere else you are out of luck. Some people might be hungry. People don't just get hungry at 8, 12, and 6. Just because someone asks you for money doesn't mean that person is trying to get a drink or buy drugs. He might really have a need. I try to help people. If they are trying to trick me, God will get them for it. But I believe he will bless me for trying to help them.

Latasha Jackson

Before becoming homeless in December of 2009, if someone came up to me asking for money, I would always without hesitation reply, "No." Then snootily go on about my business. At that time in life, I tended to in my mind clump all homeless people into one group, thinking everyone who is homeless is by choice. I thought every last one of them was a lazy drunk and addict that wanted to be homeless.

After becoming homeless myself, I became a beggar from time to time. I would bury my shame and embarrassment and I would beg for spare change or mostly bum cigarettes with blushed red cheeks. And if others asked me for money or cigarettes, if I had it I would instantly hand it over.

Now if a beggar comes up to me, if I have something to give and feel that person being truthful and won't use the money for bad, I'll give it. Also if I know the person to be an alcoholic or addict, I will refuse to give to that person. God teaches us to help, help, help the less fortunate, not to knowingly enable Satan.

Cynthia Crawford

When people come to me and ask for money, normally I'll let them know, "I'm sorry, but I don't have any," or, "I wish I had it to give you, but today I don't." Or if I have it, I just give it to them. For I know what it feels like to be hungry and lost and forgotten about.

People will see you coming and try their best not to be seen out of all sort of feelings, but I'll never know the reason why. For homeless people are usually frowned upon. Others try to hide and not help. But yet they helped to create homelessness.

When you have no job, no home - what do you do to sustain one's life? There's many ways to answer that question. For this is a deep topic, a topic of pain, hurt, confusion and, yes, it takes a lot of compassion on everybody's part to just knock a dent on it. For new faces are daily added to our homelessness. I try to be kind and caring for I know in this day and time, it does not take much to become homeless.

WJS

Before I became homeless, I was oblivious to the needs of the homeless, I'm afraid. Something as simple as using the restroom can be challenging to the homeless as there are places which only let you use the restroom if you are a customer. Also you have to rely on the kindness of others, or lack thereof, for such small things as hygiene products, which can be embarrassing at times. From my experience the best way for the homeless is to find places that help the homeless and camp out near them. It's rare that people make trips to the homeless so that's why your stuff should be near soup kitchens, places to get hygiene, etc., if at all possible depending on what city you live in. I needed clothing because I had thrown everything away when I went to the streets so I camped out around clothes closets until I had a couple of skirts stocked up and hidden in my cathole. Now that I know what the homeless need, I make it a point to fulfill the need as much as I can. But by all means, stick together with others in your situation.

Tamara Hendrix

If someone on the street asked me for money today, I would give because I understand more now what that person is going through. Before I experienced homelessness, I thought homeless people were just beggars, but now I know different. And I understand more where they are coming from. I have needed one or two dollars to make my day better. So I would give until it hurts. Being homeless changed the way I look at panhandling.

Donna Connie

Now that I am not homeless anymore, if a person asks me for money, if I have some spare change I would gladly give it to that person. Because I have experienced it first-hand and I know where the person is coming from. In a way I was glad that I was homeless at one time in my life so that I would know the difference. Because sometimes 5 or 10 dollars can mean the difference between life or death.

Leroy Scott

When I was on the street, money was given to me on a gift money card. Most of the time, I looked for jobs and received them; work a few hours to pay for a room. I did this for a year and a half. Later, I came to the Door of Hope. I would give to a homeless person so they can buy shoes and food. They are human beings and people do care about other people.

Master Major Joshua Williams

When I was homeless, I used to go in middle class neighborhoods and ask for money for different reasons. Sometimes it would be for drugs, alcohol, and food. But you realize when you was in the street, you experienced different things and learn how to deal with people in the street. When somebody asks me for change I give them change, but when they ask me for money for food, I will buy them food or give them food. When I am blessed I also bless other people. I am a giver because when I help people that are in need, I always get blessed triple from the master that is Jesus Christ.

Robbin K

I have given people money who were panhandling. That was before I realized what some of them do with the money. I hear people say that they are responsible for blessing others with the money, not what they do with it. I feel differently. When I know they are going to buy drugs or alcohol, I am enabling them. I know because I used to be one of them. I also feel bad knowing that a drink or drug I helped pay for may be the one that kills them. There are places to get food, clothes, hygiene products and shelter for free. There is even a free doctor and medication. Anyone who spends all day panhandling has the sense and energy to do a job. Too often I hear people say they won't do a job sweeping or mopping, but those same people think it's o.k. to panhandle. Panhandling should be a job so they can pay taxes and help our economy. Let's see how many career panhandlers we would have then.

Veyshon Hall

When people ask me for money in front of a grocery store, I usually recoil. If you bum enough quarters, you'll soon have enough for a beer. It's a daily routine. Bum change and buy beers. Many street people have made this their daily occupation. Sometimes I will give some change to hustlers and sometimes I won't. It's according to how I feel in a particular day, I guess. When I was homeless I worked at temp services and always had some sort of income. I never stood in front of the grocery stores and bummed change. An upstanding tramp I was. I do feel some compassion at times and will part with a dollar or more. Or just buy the beggar a beer. I know what he's after. I could have been the same way myself. But by the grace of god I survived. I don't like enabling street people to get drunk. At the same time I feel that drunkenness is their only solace from a miserable life. The same as mine was.

Tommy Payne

If someone gave me money I would be thankful even if I was given more than I asked. Sometimes I do get more than I ask. Even if I didn't ask and someone gives me money, like I said, I am thankful.

Anthony Johnston

ANTHONY JOHNSTON

I am Anthony Johnston. I was born in Jackson, Tennessee. My family lives in Middleton, Tennessee. I came to Memphis four years ago. I was without a place to live when I was 41 or 42 years old. I became homeless because I was not responsible enough to pay for a motel—I always wanted to spend money on something else. I was in and out of motels for a while. I got into housing two years ago and heard about Door of Hope through Miss June Averyt. I've been coming to writing group since 2012 when I was living down the street in an apartment complex. I keep coming to writing group because I really enjoy writing. What I like best is being together and writing. I don't find anything hard about writing group. My current favorite topic to write about is my sister and my brother. If anyone thought homeless folks in a writing group was strange, I'd tell them it's not. I'd advise others starting a writing group to keep with it (at least until you get the book written.) The most important event in my adult life was being with Betty at the art project where she taught me what I could do with art and drawing.

DEDICATION

I would like to dedicate this book to my family and especially to my sister, Mona Brady, the one that brought me up.

CHAPTER 16
THE ART OF GIVING

Thank you for your generosity
for your thoughts of helping us.
Giving and helping others
It's good to help people especially the ones who need to be helped because
we know how it is.
Giving to strangers
is showing generosity.
"Thanks again."

Anthony Johnston

Sometimes if you give, you will go on to the next thing of giving. I wanted to go past the giving and I just felt more of the giving the more I got. All my giving sometimes to get to receive a little bit. I am 50 years old and I have had things given to me more than I noticed that I was receiving. It feels better to receive than to give away. I gave a Bruce Lee story to my friend. I felt good and she promised to give me a story that she will write.

William L. Hogan, Jr.

If I receive, I feel like I have to give, especially to people that are less fortunate. When you give, God gives you more. It just makes me feel so good. When I get that happy look or that special smile, I like to receive those special blessings that only God can give. It feels great to get something back when you know you have done something good for someone else. I like receiving gifts, but I also like giving gifts. You can give people a smile, an encouraging word. You don't have to always give money. How can God give you more when you are holding on to everything?

Latasha Jackson

Some of the things I give other than money are my time, some knowledge of certain situations, physical help, looking for someone, a shoulder to cry on, running some errands for someone, being a loving father, friend, and lover.

Leroy Scott

Memphis is a lovable city (Thank God). It's nice when people are nice back, ya-no? It's a different kind of feeling, something gets warm in your heart.

Rhonda Lay

I believe in a giving way. There's a way to give and a way not to give for Seasons and reasons. Too many people are proudful and wear their feeling. I am one of the people who would spend it like it was their first and last money. I would be a giver and be proud to share an amount of cash—to bless people like the people from Germantown bless us. Thank You!

Master Major Joshua Williams

There is hope that people will have a kind heart—to be grateful in giving—and not to expect anything in return! It's better to give than to receive all the time; if a person can give a little of time—or an ear to someone, it maybe can make a difference. The hope is that people will treat each other the way they want to be treated! Because it's not all about one person or people! It's about what can we give to the world or society without taking all the time. I know it makes a person feel good about themselves and in Higher Power eyes. The Blessing that comes to someone—because they went out of their way to make sure someone else had something maybe— food, shelter, or their word. It's not all about the money all the time—it helps. But I hope we learn how & when to give.

Roderick Baldwin

What makes a person give and give when it hurts? Why do people keep neglecting themselves to give to another. Crazy, neediness, stupid, glutton for pain? Nope, I just plain can't help it. Sure I have my off days, but in the end, I'm gonna be nice. At first I couldn't explain or understand this giving/being nice madness. In the beginning it was fear. God said Love Thy Neighbor, so I did, so he wouldn't be angry. Then I learned that God is not a punishing God and I realized I actually like being nice to others. Since I know all too well how it feels to have someone be mean, I choose to be nice. I don't want them to feel sad like I used to. And besides, what real reason do I have for not being nice/generous? None. The bottom line is, it makes my spirit feel really good when I serve others. When my spirit feels good, everything is all good, God all the time.

Veyshon Hall

Santa is a gift giver!

In the Christmas season, we all get together like family and friends in being givers—presents and bags of stuff. It costs people to give gifts each year and the over special months.

Master Major Joshua Williams

I guess generosity is an inborn trait. Many people are by nature generous while many are not. I guess its all in the genes.

I admire generous people. I often wish I could have enough money to donate to charitable concerns. I'm not always generous. I sometimes hoard things like clothes. I have many items of clothing that I've never worn and probably never will wear. All of a sudden, I will chastise myself for being a hoarder and give away whole wardrobes. I guess my generosity gene is slow working. I can be a pack rat. With a room full of mementos that I have accumulated over the years. I have some vintage name brand shoes that I've kept for over 30 years. I don't wear them. I go to church in tennis shoes and sometimes old jeans. My church is come as you are. So I don't go anywhere to dress up. So what's the point of hoarding all these shoes and clothes?

Eventually my generosity gene kicks in and I realize how silly I can be and just give away most of my accumulations.

I'm not that financially stable to give away much money. But I really believe that if I was a multimillionaire I would give big sums of money to charities and foundations. It may take a while. Like I said, my generosity gene can work very slowly.

I remember the parables about blessed is the cheerful giver and you must give in order to receive. This has been the case with me. I give away a lot of things. Even my paintings. But I also come by a lot of things…so—eventually give it away. It works out fine.

Blessed is the cheerful giver! The more you give the more you receive. A true fact.

Tommy Payne

It make me feel good to give something to someone because I was without and in need for help, in need for clothes, in need for food, in need for mostly everything that you could ask for.

Jacqueline Crowder

I always feel good when I can give someone something, a dollar, some food, a nice cool drink, or whatever I have that they are in need of. I hate it when I can't give to someone in need. I like to give because God gave the most important gift, his son. Since God gave I feel like I should give also.

Latasha Jackson

I'm writing to let you know, I sincerely appreciate your generosity towards Door of Hope. I'm a person whom Door of Hope has helped to see life anew. I thank you for opening your heart and letting the love that is in you shine.

Your gift will really make a difference for several individuals. Door of Hope is not a organization that would let you down. They do exactly what their name entails. Give Hope to Individuals who society has shunned, who's trying to remake a society with a new Spirit of Hope and new directions.

It humbles me and makes me appreciate people who do show their inner being, for I once gave up on people because all I saw was their ugly side. Thank you so much for being a Restorer of Hope. And I would like to invite you to one of our writing classes if you should choose, also I extend that invitation to our next Writer's Retreat.

Sincerely and with Heart Felt thanks.

WJS

I'm sure you have heard thank you a million times. Well add a trillion to that and you will be close to the amount of times I'm thanking you. I'm a stranger, an unknown, a spot in the colored rainbow and yet you care about me. The only reason I can give for this bizarre behavior is the love of God. You have got to be super close to God and his words. I strive to reach such a height. I pray that your journey with God forever continues and I wish many many Blessings upon you, your family and all those you encounter.

Thank you for being a humble servant of God. Because Generosity is an action word.

Veyshon Hall

Santa Claus was break dancing with all of the elves. Mrs. Claus said, "Don't forget my present Big Daddy." As he drove his magic car away saying "One of these days, Thelma, you gonna get one of these (kiss, kiss) right upside your kisser." This story means what? That Santa Claus and Mrs. Claus really do live and he is real. Right, Guys?

Rhonda Lay

RHONDA LAY

I am Rhonda Lay. I was born in Florida. The most important event of my childhood was dancing lessons. I moved to Memphis when I was 8 years old. My family lives in Memphis. I am a grandmother. The most important event of my adult life has been getting off the streets. I was first without a place to live when I was 38 years old, due to having no income. I was homeless 2 months. I became homeless again for 3 years. I wasn't married the first time, but I was the second one. I was a mother. My children were 22, 10, and 11. I got into housing in 2005. I heard about the Door of Hope through the Salvation Army. I started coming to writing group in June 2012. I was then housed at the Door of Hope. I kept coming to writing group to hear others' stories. I most enjoyed the topics, staying focused. The hardest thing is writing more than one page. My favorite writing topic is homelessness. To those who think homeless folks in writing group are strange, I'd say, "We are not strange, we are just writers." I'd like to add, Thank God.

DEDICATION

First, I want to dedicate these stories to my son Michael II (a.k.a "Jenks"). He is always there for me and he is the love of my life.

I would also like to dedicate this book to Salvation Army Single Women's Lodge. They have done so much for me that I really owe them more than just this. Mrs. Iris is the love of many women. I have made her my mom because my mom has passed away. Some days she is so silly—like when we have a party she'll get out and dance with us. But when it come time to be serious Mrs. Iris knows how to get things done, and she loves to have her picture made. The second person would be Miss Cathy. She is Mrs. Iris's second hand. She is so nice and she would give you the shirt off her back and shoes off her feet (for real). Both of them together is a blessing! I will never forget them. I would do anything for them.

CHAPTER 17
FOR THE YOUNG

I would like to write about BOYS: you know how funny it is to talk about boys and have girls talking on the phone. We would tell boys, "Who do you like? I like E. Oh no! Not him." He was the cutest little thing, everybody loved him, but he picked me.

Back then we didn't have cellphones. So we would talk on that great big phone—you know one line only but we had the longest cord ever. It would go all the way down the hall into my bedroom. We would make plans to go to the skating rink. Back then there wasn't much to do. At the end of the skating, we would play around outside (kissing) and saying stupid things to each other. Boy, if I could go back to 14, I don't want to. I'll just stay 54 and look silly at that group of children that think they know everything . . .

Let children
be children!

Rhonda Lay

I would tell my fourteen year old self to strive for better grades and not be afraid to showcase my talent more. I did okay in high school, but I could have been more successful if I had pushed myself a little harder. It seems like it was easier back then to accomplish your goals, but as you get older it becomes harder. To myself I would say, you are beautiful, because at that age I felt like an awkward teen who rarely socialized. I mean I did some after-school activities but I still felt socially ostracized. Get a backbone, is what I would say to myself because in the long run you will have to have thick skin to survive what the real world throws at you.

Tamara Hendrix

When I was 14, I was carefree. I was a little wild, but I would have done some things differently. I would tell the 14 year olds of today to study hard, learn all you can while you are in school and get a good education. I would tell them to put God first. Obey their parents, prepare for the future. I would tell them to pick their friends carefully. I would tell the young girls not to have sex, and not to have a baby until they could take care of it. I would have to tell the girls that boys lie. And to protect themselves at all times.

Latasha Jackson

When I was 14, I was in school at Jewell Arts in New York. School was hard plus I had many jobs before and after school. I worked in doctor's offices and fast food places. I had a close relationship with my father and brother and sisters. I did fun things at Season Greetings and Holidays. What I did most was grow up to be responsible and to take pride in work and jobs and everything I did. There was no play around with gang members after school. I rode the bus straight to work. All my friends had big houses. They worked before school also. The don't list was so long, like we girls and boys were not to hang out, but come right home. No street sex or eating off the street, those hot dogs and pretzels. I did the home good list.

Master Major Joshua Williams.

Fourteen. What a wonderful age. No longer a baby. You are a young lady. You are a "Teenager." You are invincible, beautiful, and the bestest daughter ever.

Yea, right! Here's the truth. Right now you are the most difficult person to get along with.

Here's why. You have a kazillion choices, billions of dreams and no idea what you want to do first. Today I call this the trial and error stage. Back then it was, I'm almost 18, you can't tell me nothin'. This is the time when you try a lot of things and figure out what's good for you. You're having a rough time, I know, that's just growing pains. Keep trying new things and getting to know yourself. Don't let anyone lead you to drugs, alcohol, violence, or any other negative thing. Your parents and others have already done that for you, just ask them. They will tell you the biggest lie they ever told themselves is, it won't happen to me. You are not invincible, yes, bad things happen to teenagers too. So be careful who you hang out with. Be safe wherever you go. And remember, the "safe" text is not to keep tabs on you but to help your mom worry less. So keep your dreams alive and have fun being a teenager.

Veyshon Hall

I would tell myself that God loves me and I don't need love from men. That has been my downfall in life, looking for love from men that I didn't receive from my father who I never met until I was 15. Who still had no part of my life. Stay in school because without it life is going to be difficult. Love yourself because this is the best love you could ever receive. Remember always that God loves you.

Life seems hard but with a little work it can get better.

Hang in there.

Donna Connie

If I was 14 again, I would advise myself to be more studious in school and not to hang out with the bad boys. I was very smart in school. I could be an A student if I liked the subjects. If I didn't care for subjects like chemistry, geometry, algebra, I would cut class and go to the library and read books on subjects I found interesting; history, biology, civics, geography and science.

I lived in a semi-tough neighborhood. If you couldn't or wouldn't fight you got treated like a punk. After school I hung out in the Lemoyne Gardens Project. Drinking wine, shooting dice and chasing girls. I'd go home pretending like I was at football practice or some school function.

My parents were not that strict. They paid little attention to me. I was finally expelled from school for beating up on a teacher. Not by myself but with some of my neighborhood gang members.

My family was sort of well-to-do. So I was sent to a Catholic school. I flunked out of that environment for bad behavior. I finally graduated by G.E.D. The Board of Education was amazed at my test scores.

I don't believe I could give myself any advice. I was born a certain way. My life fulfilled itself for what it was worth. I look at successful people, some my former school mates. I don't envy them or wish I were like them. I have my own little private world. One where I can paint pictures in words and on canvases. This was perhaps my destiny. Not to be a successful person. An A student or a Rhodes Scholar. Just to be Tommy.

Tommy Payne

What I would tell myself at the age of 14 is not to get pregnant at the age of 14. Not to go on dates at an early age. My brothers and sister were very mean to me. Now that I am older I can take care of myself.

Jacqueline Crowder

When I was 14 years old, that's when they started the 9th grade to transfer as a Freshman in High School. I had 3 brothers in High School and they were athletes in track, basketball and football. Being their little sister, as they call me K.'s sister. The teacher and coaches with sports, they expected too much out of me. They put me on a pedestal and had high expectation about me. Because of my brother's talents. I had talent but everyone was always looking at me to be better in sports and everything else.

All I wanted as a 14 year old young girl was to be normal and go with CJ, because he was fine, fine. Not to be call "K's sister." I wanted to play sports and go to pajamas party, and go to Sadie Hawkins dance to have fun, and not to be torching by my brother's look and staring. Go home to tell my mother about the dance and not to argue with my brothers of what they seen me doing or not doing. I thank God to reach my age today as 45 years old.

Robbin K

I know you hear this a lot "If I knew what I know now I would be different." I would like to have a meet & greet for teens who are heading in the wrong path in life. A chance to meet someone who they may become if they don't change. Meeting people who didn't listen to their parents. And where they are because of it.

Donna Connie

Success
Success is not just about where you
end up.
Success is also about the journey and
what you learned along the way.

Success is not just about where you
have been in your past.
Success is also about where you want
to go.
Success is not just about you.
Success is also about the lives you touch along the way.
Success is not just about taking a final bow.
Success is about the steps that got you there.
Success is . . .
Seeking
Unification
Character
Commitment
Exercising
Self
Sufficiency

Cynthia Crawford

Love is kindness and sometimes you can't see it because people hide their love with not caring because of being treated bad or family problems but really they do love, because everybody is born of God and God is Love.

Anthony Johnston

The one thing I wish someone would have told me when I graduated was that I was not ending my education, I was just beginning my life lessons. When I graduated, I thought I knew a lot, but life taught me that I didn't know as much as I thought I knew. I wish someone would have told me that sometimes life would be hard. I thought that having a diploma would make it a piece of cake to just make my dreams come true, but I found out that I had to work hard to achieve them. Life has a lot of turns. Try not to make the wrong ones.

Latasha Jackson

CHAPTER 18
WORDS OF WISDOM

Being afraid only holds you back from your true blessing. Being afraid is somewhat a form of ignorance to me. Because it keeps you from striving to be the best you can be. And life is too short and too good to be missing anything in life.

I had a phobia of needles but I have spent so much time in the hospital that I no longer have that. I found out that if you just go ahead and forget it, it doesn't bother me anymore.

I found out that once you achieve Faith True Faith you really won't be afraid of too many things at all. So in ending Don't Hate!

AWAKE!!!

Feel

Say

Act

Go

Leroy Scott

Patience is the best virtue. Take it from me. I been there before.

William L. Hogan, Jr.

I am learning not to be afraid because of the journey that the Lord is leading me in the right directions of my life. Since I have been here in Memphis he is teaching me to learn and to cope with situations, that I have to confront things than to run away from the problem. My life has been a rocky mountain over 20 years of my life. So now I have to learn to face that mountain, and conquer it with eyes wide open and be obedient and have the confidence and the courage to move on and learn from it. Fear and afraid had dominated me for a long time but now I can love myself and people and even my own enemies because love conquers it all. So right now I know who I am in him. I am glad I had an eye opening experience to be able to help someone else that the things and my testimony that I put myself through have been foolish in this world.

Robbin K

Don't be afraid of new stuff in the new year. They said to be or not to be. Just because you don't know, don't be afraid. If you know, speak up and not be afraid. For I know I have to serve and I'm not afraid.

Master Major Joshua Williams

Education comes first on finding jobs. Read and find out how he or she got a job and try the same. And if finding a job, work at your best like being a writer. And that's what I want to be is a writer.

Anthony Johnston

The biggest challenge for the nation is teamwork. Countries fighting countries. States divided, neighbor against neighbor. We each have something to make this a better nation. We have to not just learn, but internalize the fact that we are equal. Race, religion, size, height, rich or poor. We all are the same inside and no matter how hard we fight it, we need each other. You can't stop war by creating a war. You can't stop hunger by being selfish. You can't lower prices by taking over a country. You can't stop crime by being a criminal with a badge. What is it going to take for us to work together? I know: God!

Veyshon Hall

In my younger years I had many expectations, both of myself and others. People had many expectations of me also. As I grew older most of these expectations failed to materialize and the few that did still did not satisfy what my intentions were.

I soon learned the hard way not to expect too much from myself or others. To adopt a pragmatic philosophy and just allow life to dictate its own course and not try to make things happen purely because I wanted them to happen. Nothing in life is guaranteed, and it is somewhat foolish to think so. I take things as they come and try to grasp opportunities when they come along while making the best of any situation. I try to look for the good in any circumstances and quickly remove myself from any situation that is not good.

Maybe its just drifting along like a bubble in the ocean or maybe its some truth in the philosophy of letting life take its own course and live one day at a time.

Expectations? All I can truly expect is for the sun to rise on the morning and the moon to come out at night.

Tommy Payne

Congratulations on running that race. It's something I hope to accomplish one day.

I know it may not have been easy but you did it. Whether or not you realize it, it took courage. Hebrews 12:1 says, "Therefore we also, since we are surrounded by so great a cloud of witnesses, let us lay aside every weight, and the sin which so easily ensnares us, and let us run with endurance the race set before us." So to me that says don't worry about the finish line, just run. It also takes faith and trusting God to finish the race or task in you and through you! I know I personally have been through a lot of struggles in my life. Struggles that may be too heavy for the next person or even a feather weight to you. But as I look back I realize there were others there with me including Jesus and God. Others who either encouraged me or perhaps carried me. Sometime I even passed the baton and later retrieved the baton on down the race way.

What I'm saying is if you have been through something, are going through something, and/or will go through something, remember you aren't alone. One day you will have a powerful testimony from this to help others as they go through things. I truly believe what doesn't kill us makes us stronger! For it isn't the fearless but the courageous who succeed!

Cynthia Crawford

If you want to know the meaning of frustration, try to wait. But at the same time waiting can be a good thing because you learn how to have faith and believe that things are going to be all right sooner or later. It also helps you to dream good thoughts and to see what and who you are dealing with close up, but the greatest thing of all is when what you waited for comes to you. There is no better feeling. It is truly a blessing.

Leroy Scott

Violence has no place in the human race. There is no need for it. If the world had no violence it would be a better place to live. A lot of the problems in the world would be solved. And a lot of great people would be here. That is a world I would love to live in. And raise the next generation in.

Donna Connie

I think that the Steve Wilkos and Jerry Springer Show should be put off of television. It's violence. Please, you acting other people, give us a peaceful show. I can't take those fights, exciting fist fight or no money. Listen, the place for that fight is jail. It's disturbing is what I say. They stay in the show seat for money, to feel tall.

William L. Hogan, Jr.

Well, to me what is in need of peace is neighborhood violence, rape, murder and gangs. What I am in need of peace personally is love for my brother and sister and the world.

What do Freedom and Peace look like? To me they look like a newborn baby, a beautiful flower, a romantic sunset, and a brand new truck.

Leroy Scott

I have been a very impatient person. And for this reason many of my dreams came to no realization. I took matters into my own hands and suffered many negative consequences for not being able to wait on god's blessings. God seems to know the exact time to bring a person into the fulfillment of that person's life. I have acted a lot of times like I didn't believe in god. No one who ever knew me during these times would have had the slightest notion that I could paint or write. Gradually god took me away from my negativity and instilled in me a sincere desire to help people and be of good service to others. Mostly through tragedies in my life. Now, I am patient. I am able to wait on god to do with me as he wills. I am thankful for this rebirth.

Tommy Payne

Change can be kind, change can be sad. Change can be horrible. Change is always a challenge to be a better person. In the last couple of years, I have been through many, many changes. Changing from an independent, outgoing, productive member of society to a semi-independent individual has been trying. At first, I was extremely angry. Then I went through the Why Me's. Finally, there is acceptance and gratitude. I'm still accepting. Some days, it's kicking and screaming and some days I'm just confused. Through all my changes God is there and my gratitude a must. No one likes change, but it has to be done to become a better person. You can change smoothly or roughly, your choice. Me, I'm going with the God flow.

Veyshon Hall

There are a lot of changes that come in to a person's life. If it's the family—the change of moving, because the kids are going to leave their friends behind, the ones they have known for years. It is hard. There is the mother going through change too; she has to leave the neighborhood she has known to have shopped and visited the other parents on a day in and night time after time. The father who has to change jobs to help the family into a better situation. Sometimes change is hard for a lot—because accepting a move or going somewhere else is not easy. I have experienced a lot of change in my life; changing of jobs. Change in someone coming in to manage a business and you don't know them. Or a change in my life of leaving one lifestyle for another. It is good; but wasn't easy. I had to come to grips with that, I had to change or my life was headed in a bad way. So change is not all that bad. But hopefully for the better.

Roderick Baldwin

Sometimes I think I'm ugly, and I wish for beauty.
And other times I get so frustrated with trying to style my unbelievably curly hair that I wish for straight hair.
At times my nose reminds me of a pig's snout, and I pray for a different one.
There are even days my weight makes me wanna cry, and I beg to be thin.
And lately loneliness comes more often so I pray for true friends to come into my life.

Then I remember God made us in His image and He said, "It is very good."
So then I think who am I to question what God created and called "very good"?
I certainly am not more qualified than God to do such things.
But what I can change is how I react to things. Then maybe all these other things will change.

Cynthia Crawford

Childhood should be celebrated to the fullest. After all, you only have one. Eighteenth birthdays are cool because you can begin to make adult choices. Twenty one, the drinking age, bring on the alcohol. Twenty five, still young, but knocking at thirty. Most youngsters think 25 is old. You know I'm old, I just said youngster. I don't make a big deal about birthdays now, I'm just grateful to make another year alive. Some say I'm old, or I have matured. I'm just real seasoned like a great steak.

Veyshon Hall

What makes birthdays so important is that each year, we get a chance to improve ourselves or our lives, each year that we are alive. Birthdays can bring reflections of the past as well as start new traditions in one's life. Birthdays can spark celebrations, like a party, or an intimate gathering of family. I will always remember birthdays as a time to go out to a special dinner at a restaurant of my choice and have a cake prepared for that day.

Tamara Hendrix

I hate change, period. I can be very satisfied in the same environment. I'm sort of like a chameleon. I change colors to melt into the background and be unnoticed. I can get along in just about any situation. I can run with the rabbits as well as the hounds. I am mutable but stationary. I never change my personality regardless of the situations.

But, one must change in order to evolve spiritually. I am still the same person but I am always seeking higher definition of myself. I am always an artist even though I have played many roles in my drama of life. I've been to the lowest as well as the highest states of being. But nothing has really changed about my personality. I am combative, volatile, and temperamental. I have had to display these characteristics on different levels. For the good and for the bad. I don't change easily. My religious beliefs have matured to be very strong and very soft. I am caught between extremes. I am empathetic and compassionate. But at the same time I can be very hostile and aggressive – a passive-aggressive personality.

But age has made me more compassionate and good thinking. Because one day I must eventually change from a flesh man into a spiritual man.

I look forward to this absolute change.

Tommy Payne

Dear Bobby,

Sitting here thinking of last night, even though it happened to have a somewhat bad situation for me, you, and Sherie, I believe we can overcome this enigma. I feel that living the way we are, we must practice self control and more thinking about pleasant futures because Lord knows we been through Hell and Back and back again.

As I sit here thinking how a small problem almost cost me a very important friend, it really bothers me because to find a real friend and to be able to keep that friend I believe is a God sent thing and I intend to keep this friendship for as long as I live. And I hope you feel the same.

Leroy Scott.

If you go into a space, how to get noticed? You sometime tell your name, but if you just would have good health or show a vision you have, then this will make you stand out around someone. Just if you were add to sports, you would be healthy and going at showing that something. Or control the time with your mind to be full of spirit showing your figure muscles or longness tall big or with a little you

would feel better and become a step closer to a happy spirit.
William L. Hogan, Jr.

What is happening with nature? We practically skipped winter, spring, sprouted summer and thunderstorms are roaring through the nation. The flowers and trees are blooming not just budding. The animals are confused and they look terrified. Are you afraid? Are you wondering what's going on? Nope. Everybody is going on through life ignoring God. That's right, ignoring God. The book of Revelations tells the truth of the end of the beginning. I'm not afraid, because I have been working toward everlasting life. I'm not perfect, just humble and obedient. Are you prepared? Are you getting ready? The clock is running out, tag—you're it.
Veyshon Hall

A family is your loved ones (or at least they are supposed to be). A family can be your church family. A family can be a group of friends who live with you. Sometimes your (blood) family can betray you, and make you feel like a stranger instead of family. You can marry into a family and they can become your family. Sometimes your family is the friends that you are around from day to day. They can be like a support group.
Latasha Jackson

Is love a red rose or a blue violet? I say it is not. I say love is the care that goes into raising those flowers. Just like the love put forth to raise a child. Oh, love, as Shakespeare once wrote, let me count the ways! Love is not just saying, I love you! But it's an action, something you do which shows love. And also more than that, GOD is love, beyond all earthly understanding. He loved us enough to create us. As Psalm 139 sings, he knit each one of us together in our mother's womb. He knows our very marrow, every cell. He loves us so much he came to earth clothed in an earthly body to meet us on our level and died for us all so that we might be born again if we choose him. To die to our earthly self and live for him. Then we will have eternal life with him, our creator.

Cynthia Crawford

Today is a good day about our new president. I can see the economy changing and people are focus on housing, jobs and blessings. God is not going to let his people suffering and in every generation he raise up a prophet to change things. We need to stick together and love one another and give charity back to the community. If we come together in unity is power. We don't know how things going to be or turn out to be. But we have to step in faith and believe that god can do anything he please to do. We have to learn obedience and learn how to deal with situation in our life. We can do anything we want to do if we can come together as a nation in unity.

Robbin K

If you could have God change one thing about human beings, what would it be? First and foremost would be the search for truth and honesty to see more with our hearts instead of our eyes. Have more compassion for our brother man.

Leroy Scott

There are people, according to psychiatrists, who suffer from a mental disorder that makes them prone to see everyone else as inferior to themselves. They are called "labelers." No matter how creative and intelligent a person may be they will be looked upon in a negative manner. Just because they may have used drugs or went to jail.

Psychiatrists say that labeling is a form of social chastisement for people who don't or didn't come up to the self righteous standards of society. No matter what adjustments a person makes to the particular behavior, the label sticks. So, Betty Ford will always be a drug addicted first lady. George Bush will always be a draft dodging alcoholic. Perhaps I will always be a crack smoking homeless thief who sleeps in "cat holes." No matter what adjustments I have made to my lifestyle.

The point is that the labelers are just as mentally maladjusted as the ones they label.

If you see a person down in the dirt, flat on his or her face, try to pick them up. Don't label them as a dirt eater. Then sniggle about their predicament

I often visit a "cathole." A three bedroom, two bath, patio, cable, air conditioned cat hole. Cupcake, Funny Face and Panther are the main cats. With about 6 other of their friends. I love cats. They are always welcome where I may take a nap.

Tommy Payne

"What is a True Leader?"
A true leader is not just someone
who talks or instructs, but
the one who walks the walk.
A leader may not always be popular
but that perseverance makes great
character.
A leader can be old, young, or anywhere
in between.
Being a leader isn't always easy.
Pushing through the pain and difficulty
is a mark of a true leader.
And I believe it should be a qualification.
A true leader is . . .
Tactful
Respectful
Unique
Experienced
and
Learned
Exciting
Appreciative
Dedicated
Effervescent
Reliable

Cynthia Crawford

The very first time you cough and choke,
Your friends find that a hilariously funny joke.
The second is euphoria, a meshing of you two,
It feels so good, you finish it all the way through.
By the third time, it's off to the races,
As you continue to blow smoke in everyone's faces.
They ask, "What is this fantastic thing you have found?"
"Please. Come see," you say as they gather round.
Then suddenly the screaming begins,
As you look at the horrified faces of your friends.
"What is it?" What do you see?
The answer in unison, "Lung Cancer, Heart Failure, and Liver
Disease."
It is destroying and killing all that you are,
Just so you can be a Cigarette/Cigar star!

Veyshon Hall

People need help with their smoking hunger. Take for instant that
I used to get in my eye a camera to smoke just a ¼ of the cigarette. I
smoke a 1/2 of a cigarette, and all of a sudden I had got control over
my smoking. I know if the street cure can't give you a cigarette out
there with that sidewalk save this is the method. Be important about
your smoking. Keep like a date—yes, you are dating a girl. Try a ¼
count. It will save you. Remember you can make this play like the
game of football. Play some the games and smoke ¼ and it will be all
better and you can be a winner.

William L. Hogan, Jr.

Politically correct social groups, extremely rich people, people who
brunch. This is generally the type to eat this food. It comes in jars,
cans and plastic tubes, too. You eat it with crackers, cheese while
drinking wine. Caviar, eel, fish eggs. Who's freaky idea was that? What
weirdo said, hmmm, fish eggs, yummy! Well, I haven't ever tried them
and don't see it happening, but good eating to you.

Veyshon Hall

The weirdest food that I can't believe people eat is pig's (or any animal's) testicles. I don't understand why people would think that it would be good or even sound good to eat. I have seen them prepared and I still don't think you could make them smell or taste good—even if you were a professional chef, you couldn't.

Tamara Hendrix

I am a great vegetable eater. Usually people like to eat meat and pay very little attention to vegetables. I like squash, okra, peas, beans, corn, even rutabagas and turnips. I can even eat vegetables with the absence of meat. I like the feeling of being healthy. Once I learned that vegetables were more healthy to eat than meats, it only affirmed my already liking for vegetables.

Of course I like meats also. But I tend to stick to chicken and fish. Once I learned that red meats, beef and pork, were high in cholesterols and saturated fats and they led to high blood pressure and strokes, I almost weaned myself away from too much red meats. I almost forgot to mention cabbages, tomatoes, radishes, cantaloupes, water melons, grapes, peaches, pears, oranges and apples.

I am a health nut and it seems to have paid off very good. I'll be 66 this year, and I'm still getting a lot of exercise, but I owe my good health to eating lots of vegetables, fruits, and a little wine or beer to go along with them.

Tommy Payne

I have always enjoyed exercise and to a great extent eating healthy. I can honestly say being homeless has not affected my ability to exercise. My favorite form of exercise is and always has been simply walking. Being outside, people watching, bird watching and just feeling a true connection with Mother Nature is very relaxing and encouraging at the same time. It's been proven a body in motion stays in motion and a body at rest tends to stay at rest. I have proved this to myself. The more I sit, the more I have to sit. But the more I walk, the more I have to walk. So for me it's just a matter of staying active.

Similarly, the more unhealthy food I eat, the more I crave unhealthy food and junk food. The more water I drink, the more water I crave.

Cynthia Crawford

There is a lot of books out there that help people with certain things in their life, from creating life, building things, down to maintaining what you have. But there is a book that helps a person, especially in developing a sense of direction the person can live a positive life & have an attitude; that is wholesome for life. Not everyone believes in this book; if they just give it a chance, maybe we have a more peaceful world. It's easy said, that done.

The book has helped me in my journey, to be a better person. It helps in understanding of powerlessness, forgiving, open minds, but to obey the laws of nature. We have been given direction on how to live. But it's up to us. I believe in it; it has made me an example in life. So when my Book of Life is written, in the end; it will say well done— well done!

Roderick Baldwin

Death is a topic that is rarely discussed. It's like a social taboo to objectively confront this utter reality. It overwhelms the mind and shatters the emotions. Some people never recover from the death of a loved one. The finality of death can be totally excruciating.

Strangely, when a loved one dies from old age, the pain is much easier to bear than when a loved one dies suddenly or tragically. At least from my personal experience. My grandmother lived to be 103 while my mother died at 62 from a gunshot to the head. I experienced very little grief from my grandmother's death but was totally devastated with my mother's death. When life is cut short by an act of violence, an incurable disease, or a tragic accident, death has a greater sting. When a loved one dies peacefully having lived a full life, grief is overcome by fond memories of the beloved.

It's not the same.

Be thankful for whatever life bestows upon you. Find happiness in simple terms. Nourish the soul by refining the personality and the ego to enhance humanism. We are all created equal. God planned it that way. The rich must die the same as the poor. Death is an equalizer. What happens after death is judgement and accountability. If god has the power to create us from nonexistence, then why has he not the power to raise us from the dead and hold us accountable for our earthly deeds?

We borrow life from god. We do not own it. What we do with it is left up to the individual.

I philosophize too much. I pontificate too much. I talk too much. I guess this is my calling. As well as my downfall.

Let go and let god. Is simple enough. But I wouldn't be a writer if I didn't explore the usages of grammar and make a sing song symphony out of a simple topic.

Let go and let god is what I have been trying to say.

Tommy Payne

There is just something about sitting down to a hot meal that warms and relaxes the soul and brings people together. Some of the best conversations I've been a part of in my life have been at dinner tables. There is also something about the dinner table that brings up subjects that people would never bring up and talk about anywhere else. Let's be honest—who really wants to know about how Dad laid a 20-something-year-old waitress? Or about years ago when Granny had multiple orgies? We also don't care about how Great Aunt Brenda got a yeast infection from a toilet seat. Yeah, right—as if that's really possible!

Another thing that brings us together is the death of a loved one. Some come to make sure the person really is dead. Others genuinely want to mourn. Then there are the culprits that just want to inherit something or just use it to their advantage.

Cynthia Crawford

I like my freedom. The country is put together by freedom. Instead of fighting, the president ought to tell the other countries his government means freedom to operate. That President Bush now need to go inside people of his country and tell them it's now freedom time for the single man to just release himself or people. This would open a whole new situation around us.

William L. Hogan, Jr.

CHAPTER 19
POLITICS AND THE POOR

The congressmen are trying to keep us working till we are 80. They gotta be kidding. I can imagine going to a fast food restaurant seeing a old person being propped up on a stand, cooking fries or flipping burgers. They might come to the drive-through window smiling and forget to have their dentures in. Then when you order they might get the order wrong because they forgot to put their hearing aid on. Then they finally get the order right. It might take 1 hour to get it because the cook took 35 minutes to get back from the bathroom. I hope she didn't forget to wash her hands.

Latasha Jackson

Being President is harder than anyone can imagine. If I was president, my first duty would be to reinstate prayer in school and anywhere else it's banned. People should be allowed to pray anywhere, any time, as long as it causes no harm to themselves or others. My next duty would be the biggest feeding in history, after Jesus of course. People think better on a full stomach. Then I would educate the world. Education is one of the keys to success. There are thousands of jobs, just not enough educated people to fill them. Now the nation needs more than this, but it's a good start.

Veyshon Hall

If I was in charge of the budget, I would take a look at the very special needs of this city. Like assistance on helping the poor with cost of medical care & meds. Also look into sharing the monies with agencies that help the people in need! Also look at what monies can be used in clean-up the city neighborhoods. Look at the budget and see what are the very important needs for all of the people; not just the special interest. Look at where is all the tax money going! Times are hard, but sure there is a way to spend money in the right places. I would form a committee on looking what are the most poor people & things in this needs the monies to help out or get things headed in the right direction.

Roderick Baldwin

My thoughts as far as the government and taxes, I could write a whole book about this. But I'm not going to bore you. President Obama has done a wonderful job trying to help America. Our country has been through so much as far as bringing our soldiers home, lowering and raising our taxes. This is not something that can be fixed in one term. When it took time so little to mess up royally.

Jacqueline Crowder

The greatest challenge that our country faces is unemployment. I have not had a job in 5 years. It was already hard for me to find a job because I have little education, but now it is impossible. I just want to be able to work and take care of myself. The world is worse because there are no jobs.

Donna Connie

Never in this country's history has there not been national debt. Rich corporations, multi-national banks, etc., always gain tax cuts and tax shelters. The burden of debt is not laid upon them but on the poor, the disabled, and the mentally challenged. In the Bible, in Daniel's vision he saw a huge figure in the shape of a man. This figure had a head, neck, and shoulders of gold. A breast area of silver, a copper abdomen, and legs of iron. Quite an impressive figure. But what made this figure so weak it had feet of gross metal and clay. What Daniel was getting at is the class system of many modern civilizations. The rich upper classes- the head, breasts, and abdomen areas of the figure - were supported by the weak crumbling feet. The poor carry the burdens of the lavish economic structure. We get our own little scraps from the rich man's table and make out the best we can. Now Republicans want to take even our scraps away. Daniel predicted that this figure would crumble and fall. Because its feet could not support the upper parts of its body. If the poor fall, the entire social structure will fall on any modern terms. Stock market crashes. The poor must be propped up to maintain the rich. They must be strengthened to support our nation. "Obama care," Republicans call it. Obama has a biblical sense of reason. Nation debt? Who is going to make us pay it? China? Saudi Arabia? Peru? We are the same imperialistic conquerors we always were. Our military is too overwhelming. We'll pay when we get ready to pay. That may be a hundred years from now. Republicans, he is for real! Support the poor and stand on solid feet.

Tommy Payne

I think it is terrible that America (the greatest country in the world) is about to default on our loan and ruin our good credit. I don't understand why they (the Congress and Senators) can't work together to get the budget fixed. I know they are going to be trying to start cutting from the poor. They always want to take from the people who need it the most. I bet, if they gave up those raises every year, the debt would go down a lot. But we know they are not going to do that. If some people can make it on $200 a month, why can't they make it on what they make without having to get a raise every year?

Latasha Jackson

If I was elected president I would put together new jobs and put together Medicaid for the poor and strive forward in what you want to accomplish, and make sure the homeless have a home to go to. That's what I would do.

Jacqueline Crowder

In my experience as a senior citizen my biggest challenge is health care. The prescription drug plans are off the chain, so are co-payments. Prescriptions are too high so that drug plans really don't cover enough of the cost. The ambulance rides are too high, and x-ray's and special services are too high and they expect you to pay those bills out of the small Social Security checks that you get every month. It makes it almost impossible, plus it helps ruin the little credit that you do have.

Social Security raises are few and far, but health care is rising daily. So I pray that the fat cats would please give the hard working little guys a break and a real chance to enjoy last days. It would be a much better society in which to live.

Leroy Scott

My pastor is the most excellent young man I have ever listened to. He is making us aware of a heresy that has pervaded Christianity for over 20 years now. "The Gospel of Prosperity."

Even our economic system reflects these heretical teachings. The government has threatened to default on its promises to the disabled, the poor, and our retirees while it seeks to gain more tax cuts and incentives for the rich corporations.

The pastor noted how the prophet Amos condemned Israel for the same practices. Amos predicted that Israel would become destitute and lose its military supremacy as a result of its lavish wealth while the poor, the disabled, the sick, the old, were oppressed and downtrodden.

The question is should we allow rich corporations and multinational banks to get away without paying fair taxes and take away the little measly 7 or 8 hundred dollars a month we, the poor, must survive on?

The ghost of Amos cries out from the grave. This prediction concerning Israel became true.

When the banks and corporations defaulted, Obama bailed them out. The poor are only asking to keep our scraps from the rich table. To pay our rent and have bus fare. Maybe a little fun.

But the rich have been known to use scare tactics on the poor. We, the poor, have been known to waste our earnings (or stipends) on drugs and alcohol.

I'm just looking at both sides of the issue.

Maybe Israel saw the same issues. As a Presbyterian—whatever. I say both the rich and the poor have the same moral and social responsibilities. To act in good faith and use good judgement about what we do with our money.

Tommy Payne

I think Memphis is great because we have government that leads the city to good jobs and work. We don't have the rank of a city with a crime rate is very high. It is a city that you can take care of yourself in. It is a moderate city which has a good school system and plenty of career options. We are set up on taxes. I have made a pretty good life here and remember the time of the past in which the children of the future can make footsteps in a direction to a good life and stand tall in the city.

William L. Hogan, Jr.

If you could meet one of these persons from the past or present, who would you choose and why? My choice would be Abraham Lincoln because I would like to know how he really felt about black people as real people. Because back in those days whites looked at people by color and nothing else. Blacks weren't a part of the law making process or anything else that mattered. I would like to know to what extent his compassion went and why, because everyone else mostly looked at us as cattle or something or somebody to use or misuse.

Leroy Scott

The man that said that slavery was a blessing in disguise for African-Americans needs a lesson in history. The history of the slave trade is the darkest era in human civilization. Slavery has been a social institution since the beginnings of organized societies, but the African slave trade was the most brutal in history. It is estimated that at least 25 million slaves died in the trek from the interior of Africa to the waiting ships on the coast. Then, only one in ten slaves survived to reach the New World. Being packed like sardines on slave ships took a dreadful toll in human lives. Not slave lives—human lives. It was recorded that human skulls at the port to Zanzibar prevented the slave ships from entering the harbor. Slaves were boated to the ships. We are talking about millions of skulls in the water. Slave children roamed the backs alleys of Zanzibar searching for mothers they would never see again. They died from starvation only to be eaten by rabid dogs. This was the heart of darkness—a stark reminder that civilization was built upon merciless evil and human sacrifice.

African-Americans are the survivors of a holocaust. Once freed from slavery, we had to still fight for civil rights and equality. We are stereotyped as being shiftless and lazy, drunkards and pimps, studs and freeloaders, nymphos and whores. Slavery is no blessing by any standard, at least not to the slaves. The man who said that needed to say that slavery was a blessing to the slave owners. People made rich by slave labor.

Tommy Payne

CHAPTER 20
YET TO COME

Now that I have gotten stable I am trying to go back to school so that I will have a better life. I am trying to get a better job so that I can move forward.

I think that the next step for me would be to start to find the school that I want to attend. Then I have to go take the entrance test and after that I have to get my funding started. Then I'll be ready to start my schooling. Then I can get a better house.

Latasha Jackson

Born in Arkansas, raised in New York and now living in Memphis. They say, "Home is where the heart is." What does that mean? My heart hasn't ever felt home anywhere. That's why owning a house has always been my dream. There have been so many obstacles to that goal and more to come I'm sure. I'm not going to give up on that dream because I don't know how. It's like my heart knows that one day I will be able to say Home Sweet Home, and mean it.

Veyshon Hall

It is my dream to help the less fortunate through continuing a program of a 12 step housing. There are so many agencies out there! But with my dream, I would use any resources to continue in helping the individual who has no place to go. Come to my house, get the special support. As a person who has been homeless, maybe with the resources, I can be there to help someone to help better their situation, like food and a safe haven.

Roderick Baldwin

I was born in Memphis and finished High School at Melrose in Orange Mound. What I would like to change about me is today I would go to a four-year college, finish, and then get a job. Get married and then have two children. Buy a house, a car, and some day open up my own business.

Jacqueline Crowder

I would like to take my patience, kindness and joy with me in the new year. These gifts helped me sustain in 2012, so it's only right that I bring them to 2013. Also I would like to work on my spiritual gifts, singing for the Lord, praying in the Spirit, and reading the Bible. I believe that 2013 is the year of changes and new beginnings (well, every new start to a new year is if you want it to be).

Tamara Hendrix

If I could just get on the road and go, I would pack up an RV and the kids and take a 2-year tour of America. Enjoy all the sights, sounds, and smells from Florida to Maine and head west all the way to California.

My first stop would be Orlando. I would treat the babies to the DisneyWorld theme park. Let 'em enjoy the food, rides, and games. I can just imagine Cinderella greeting my girls. My girls would blush, giggle, and charm her right out of her jeweled crown! I can also see myself and the boys riding in the famous teacup ride, giggling enough to almost wet our pants!

From there we would hit all the beaches of Florida and the Carolinas. Even visit the famous Times Square in New York City. Then taste one of those famous hotdogs sold at a roadside stand. From there I would like to go to Olean, NY, where my dad's family lives. I would meet my Grandpa Giovanni and aunts and uncles for the first time ever. Then it's on to Rhode Island, Massachusetts, and even Maine where we would go fishing and hiking and even taste their fresh seafood and lobster. Then we would hit Pennsylvania and explore the Hershey's Chocolate Museum. Eat so much chocolate we would want to puke! Let's not forget seeing the Great Lakes and Niagara Falls, feeling the spray and mist on our faces.

We would be like gypsies wandering from tourist towns to holes-in-the-walls. Eat, sleep, and drive dependent on only each other, the RV, and GOD.

Working our way through the center of the USA, we would hit Lambert's Restaurant in the Missouri boot heel. They are famous for the throwed rolls, and we would see which of us could catch the most. Eventually we would hit the Grand Canyon, Salt Lake City, and yes even Las Vegas. No, I will not tell you what we would do there. Because remember, "What happens in Vegas stays in Vegas."

Then, no matter what, we would go to Hollywood, CA, where we would attend an actual taping of, "The Price Is Right." Of course my contagious bubbly personality would earn me a spot to be a contestant. I would win my way onto the stage and win everything right down to a double showcase.

Then I would tour Oakland, CA, where I was born. Volunteer in their soup kitchens all up and down the coast. Meeting movie stars, tramps, and, yes, even thieves. Fall asleep next to campfires while roasting marshmallows and hotdogs.

Rounding out the trip we would tour Texas. Galveston would be another beach where we would lounge, sunbathe, and swim.

At last we would end up back in Memphis, TN. We would take a tour of Memphis too. See things we had so long taken for granted and learn more of our history that perhaps we had forgotten.

Cynthia Crawford

Wild wishes are to do what I have not done, just to have a house in Memphis, for a friend, to invite a friend over for a night. Try to enjoy the city of Memphis and other places. To wish for a large amount of money and a bank account. To be a night driver and have a car and make it back safe. To live and let live and not cry about a relationship gone bad. A wild wish to know and always know.

Master Major Joshua Williams

Work I'm not familiar with. I have worked maybe two years of my 37 years of life. I quit school in the 5th grade. So I never could get a job worth working, mainly fast food, warehouse, temp work. I would love to get a degree so I could get a job I like. I have always been a worker for God. Trying to do what is right by people. When you work hard, you can play hard.

Donna Connie

I miss Mexican food. I can't afford to go to the restaurant and buy Mexican food every day so it's only when there's a special occasion that I treat myself to Mexican food. I like the different textures, spices that Mexican food has in it. My favorite foods are enchiladas. I try to make the at-home kits but nothing is better than to get them prepared at a restaurant.

Tamara Hendrix

Well, at this point and time in my life my health is binding me. You see, I suffer from congestive heart failure, asthma and chronic sleeping disorder but with the help of God and my friends and associates at the Door of Hope it is bearable.

I find that helping others also helps in my coping with my situation. I guess I could think of other things that bind me but my complaints.

Leroy Scott

We can make the changes that need to be made. We can end homelessness. We can lower the unemployment rate in Memphis. We can stop the violence that plagues our city. We can end poverty and despair. We can do anything we put out hearts and mind to do.

So when are we going to put our hearts and minds on working together so that we can make a difference?

Veyshon Hall

I wish they had a man or woman who I could get information from. He would answer questions and they would have a set up and give out writing to know what the community people need to have communicated to them. He would have a subject that I and the people could agree upon. Be able to sense his people and had an interest of social peace and order, they would be personal to your need had an interest of the body. They would get to answer most questions, give you something to get you involved in, and get you something to do. They would make the subjects of good and formula topics, and you could want and get them to stand up for you.

A Community Leader.

William L. Hogan, Jr.

I had a great but different Valentine's Day. Unfortunately, I was in the hospital 3 days prior. I experienced shortness of breath this weekend and felt very bad but I felt good that I was at the Door of Hope when my breath went short because I was among friends who cared and I had a safe feeling around me. So for my Valentine's present I was released from the hospital, and I feel a lot better now.

Leroy Scott

I took courses in journalism over 40 years ago but I have never successfully written anything of importance except for charters and racial activism. This is not my line of writing, essentially. I like writing poems, historical comments and colorful characterizations about people I have met in life.

My next step is to perhaps write an autobiography or someone else's biography. I like to elaborate on certain topics. Hopefully I will be successful.

Tommy Payne

I can visualize myself at 50 or 60 being that "crazy cat lady." I just love fluffy cats. The way they rub up against you, begging to be loved on and cuddled. They also know how to leave you alone when you don't want to be bothered. I can imagine maybe 5 feline friends prancing around my home with their noses in the air and tails pointed straight up to heaven. They leap from couch to shelf then to a table. I'll have scratch posts and cat houses randomly placed all around my house. I'll even have tons of bird houses posted all over my back yard. I'll sit on my back patio with a fresh glass of iced tea watching the cats dart after the birds, and birds will toy with and irritate the cats.

Cynthia Crawford

If I had 24 hours to live I believe I would try to talk to everyone I loved and cared about. I would do some serious praying. Give away all my possessions to everyone it could help. Go to church, take care of all my funeral fussiness, eat my favorite last meal, and pray that all mankind as well as myself be blessed and have a happy life.

Leroy Scott

CHAPTER 21
REMEMBERING THOSE ONCE IN OUR GROUP

ROBB PATE: WRITING GROUP FOUNDING MEMBER

You never know a person until you have met them, get to know their name—and have conversation with them. I met Robb Pate about 3 years ago at the Door of Hope, a very interesting man who had gotten set in believing in the Lord Jesus Christ—and Elvis Presley, the way he walked and talked—the Spirit of the Lord (kind & nice & polite), a great singer. Building relationships with people, Robb made it easy for me to do that. He helped me understand how to help people unconditionally. There was a connection with Robb where we each offered respect and had some of the same beliefs! Having a friendship like what I had with Robb is God-given! We connected spiritually, there was warmness about him. People loved him for he was a showman—an advocate for what he believed in. I know I am going to miss him. But leaving a positive spirit behind, powerful. It was an honor and a pleasure to have been part of his life.

Love you, Robb Pate

Thank God for you—in helping me on my path in life!

Roderick Baldwin

Rob Pate was one of a kind. He had a very unique personality. He was audacious as well as witty. Religion was his greatest calling. His insight into the teachings of Christ were very profound for a man of humble means and very little education.

Rob Pate was a Beale Street icon. His impersonation of Elvis Presley was remarkable. He had that smooth but gutsy voice that made

Elvis Presley famous. Rob chose a musical idol to impersonate and did a good job of capturing Elvis Presley's style.

Other than that he was a very fancy dresser. Like his idol. It took a lot of nerve to don some of Rob's costumes. Very flamboyant he was, as well as spiritual minded.

We will miss Rob Pate a lot. May heaven be his eternal resting place. We salute you, Rob, for being yourself and loving god.

Tommy Payne

I see Robb walking the sidewalks. I see him talking, head down, watching where he's going. I see him singing at church, that tiny moment of self-consciousness right before he segues into his Elvis ending. I see him, and I miss him so badly. Robb was my friend. He was probably more important to me than I was to him, and that's okay. I was crazy about Robb, and I will cherish the images I have of him, the time we spent together, the words he released into the world. I will miss you Robb, until we meet again.

Ellen Morris Prewitt

Robert Eugene ("Elvis) Pate, age 62, passed away at his home on June 12, 2010. He grew up in Columbus, Georgia where he was raised by his Aunt Dorothy. At the age of twelve, he accepted the Lord as his Savior and was baptized at Grace Baptist Church. He graduated Perry Business College and held his first job as a civilian service worker in the Airborne Training Division at Fort Benning, Georgia. He moved with his wife, Verna, to Memphis in 1999, where he found the musical atmosphere ideal for a singer/songwriter. He worked as an Elvis impersonator on Beale Street and considered his singing ability a gift from God. He loved the music of many artists. His first musical influence was Hank Williams, Jr. singing, "I Saw the Light." Elvis Presley was his favorite singer of all time, and he considered Johnny Horton a particular favorite as well. He was widowed on September 12, 2000. He was a regular columnist in the Door of Hope Newsletter, as well as a contributor to the Door of Hope Advocate. He was a member of the Door of Hope Writing Group. He was an original attendee at the Door of Hope Community Writers Retreat. In 2010, he was the co-leader of the "Writing the Spirit" workshop at the Door of Hope's 2nd Annual Community Writers Retreat. He was a life-long learner who read and wrote science fiction. His faith in God was integral to his life. He was beloved by many in Memphis, and much of his singing, writing, and acting can be found on the internet. He looked for the hidden blessing in what might have first seemed adversity and dreamed of an end to racial prejudice world-wide. He was preceded in death by his wife, Verna Ruth; his father, Robert Eugene Bullard, Sr.; and his mother, Tonie Audrey Coulter Bullard. Services will be held at St. Mary's Episcopal Cathedral on July 12 at 2:00.

LEROY SCOTT: WRITING GROUP FOUNDING MEMBER

After the compilation of this book, Leroy Scott passed from this earth. While Leroy is no longer with us physically, his spirit lives on between these pages. Thank you, Leroy—we love you.

A SPECIAL NOTE

In 1994 I fell in love with learning about homelessness and mental health. Over the years, both in formal school situations and shelters and on the streets, I have had many excellent teachers, some of whom have contributed to this book. I am deeply grateful to them and to all who have enriched my life beyond measure.

June Mann Averyt, PhD

ACKNOWLEDGEMENTS

The Writing Group would like to thank:

The volunteer typists who took our handwritten pages and typed them up: Blake Burr, Emma Connolly, Rick DeStefanis, Vena Cava, Brooke Sarden, Beverly Dorsey, Susan Yates, Shannon Maltby, Hannah's friend Benjamin, and Porsha Goodman.

Mrs. Vicki Sturdivant Stokes, author of Ms. V's Chocolate Tea Room, who spoke at our Book Retreat.

Cory Prewitt, our amazing photographer.

Robin Borczon, Blake Burr, Emma Connolly, Kristen Bernhardt, and Gabe Horton who edited the individual contributions of the writers and met with them to present the first typed-up version of the manuscript.

Barbara Vann, who offered her proofreading services.

Andy Jacuzzi, the Executive Director at the Door of Hope, who found our cover artist and lunch for our Book Retreat and so much more. He is also credited with the beautiful photographs of flowers used in lieu of authors' portraits.

Richard Smith, Don Rhoads, and the rest of the clergy and staff at Germantown United Methodist Church who hosted our Book Retreat, secured a benefactor to underwrite the publication of our book, and believed in the book until it came into being.

Martha Burkhead, Jennifer Hagerman, Haden Lawyer, and Taylor Cates for their invaluable legal assistance.

Allison Lawyer, who did the original artwork for our front cover and the interior illustrations.

Tommy Payne, who did the original artwork for our back cover.

Marilyn Hughes for organizing our first publicity event.

Michael Thompson for advice on marketing firms.

The Center for Transforming Communities and Amy Moritz who first introduced the writing group to Germantown United Methodist Church.

Our publisher, Triton Press.

The Rev. Joe Porter without whom there would have been no Door of Hope Writing Group.

INDEX OF AUTHOR BIOGRAPHIES